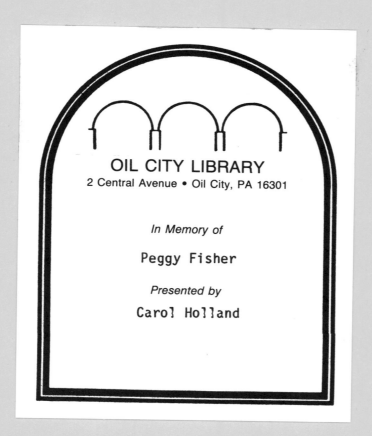

555 Little Sayings in Cross-Stitch

Marie Barber

Sterling Publishing Co., Inc. New York
A Sterling/Chapelle Book

Chapelle Ltd.

Owner
Jo Packham

Editor
Karmen Quinney

Staff
Ann Bear, Areta Bingham, Kass Burchett, Rebecca
Christensen, Brenda Doncouse,
Dana Durney, Marilyn Goff, Holly Hollingsworth,
Susan Jorgensen, Barbara Milburn, Linda Orton,
Leslie Ridenour, Cindy Stoeckl, Gina Swapp

Photographer
Kevin Dilley/Hazen Photography Studio

Library of Congress Cataloging-in-Publication Data Available

Barber, Marie.
    555 little sayings in cross-stitch / Marie Barber.
      p. cm.
    Includes index.
    ISBN 0-8069-4849-3
    1. Cross-stitch--Patterns. 2. Quotations, American. I. Title.

TT778.C76 B355 2000
746.44'3041--dc21
10 9 8 7 6 5 4 3 2 1   99-056910

Published by Sterling Publishing Company, Inc.,
387 Park Avenue South, New York, NY 10016
© 2000 by Chapelle Limited
Distributed in Canada by Sterling Publishing
⅝ Canadian Manda Group, One Atlantic Avenue, Suite 105
Toronto, Ontario, Canada M6K 3E7
Distributed in Great Britain and Europe by Cassell PLC
Wellington House, 125 Strand, London WC2R 0BB, England
Distributed in Australia by Capricorn Link (Australia) Pty
Ltd. P.O. Box 6651, Baulkham Hills, Business Centre, NSW
2153, Australia
Printed in Hong Kong
All Rights Reserved

Sterling ISBN 0-8069-4849-3

Every effort has been made to acknowledge the
sources of the sayings featured in this book. The
sources were either unknown, anonymous, or the
following: Peggy Hardman (pg. 6), Epicurus (pg. 8)
John Greenleaf Whittier (pg. 9), Adapted from
Edgar Lee Masters (pg. 12), Carl Jung (pg. 17),
Anthony J. D'Angelo (pg. 21), Isiaha 40:8 (pg. 25),
Mother Teresa (pg. 26), Emma Goldman (pg. 27),
John Sinor (pg. 46), Ralph Waldo Emerson
(pg. 46), Yiddish proverb (pg. 47), Ogden Nash
(pg. 53), Gay Talbot-Boassy (pg. 54), Elizabeth
Barrett Browning (pg. 54), Knights of Pythagoras
(pg. 62), Josephine Alexander (pg. 63), Corneille
(pg. 63), Richard L. Evans (pg. 65), Ralph Waldo
Emerson (pg. 65), Alan Jay Lerner (pg. 68),
H. Jackson Browne Jr. (pg. 69), Mother Teresa
(pg. 72), William Shakespeare (pg. 76), Edgar Lee
Masters (page 82), David Viscott (pg. 86), Dag
Hammarskjold (pg. 87), Albert Einstein (pg. 91),
Elizabeth Barrett Browning (pg. 119).

If you have any questions or comments, please
contact: Chapelle Ltd., Inc., P. O. Box 9252
Ogden, UT 84409 (801) 621-2777 • FAX (801)
621-2788 • E-mail Chapelle1@ aol.com

About the Author

Marie Barber, born and raised in Kristianstad, Sweden, now lives in Ragland, Alabama, on the Coosa River with her husband and their three children.

Marie says she has always loved to draw and illustrate. At the age of 14, she was the youngest student to study oil painting under the instruction of the late Dr. Göran Trönnberg.

She came to the United States in 1983 as an exchange student, and in 1987, returned after being accepted to the Art Institute of Atlanta. She has freelanced as a novel illustrator for a Swedish weekly publication and her artwork is featured at Loretta Goodwin's Gallery in Birmingham, Alabama. Although she has explored several avenues of the art world, Marie says she found her passion in 1993 when she began designing cross-stitch patterns.

Contents

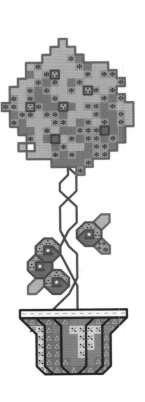

Friendship

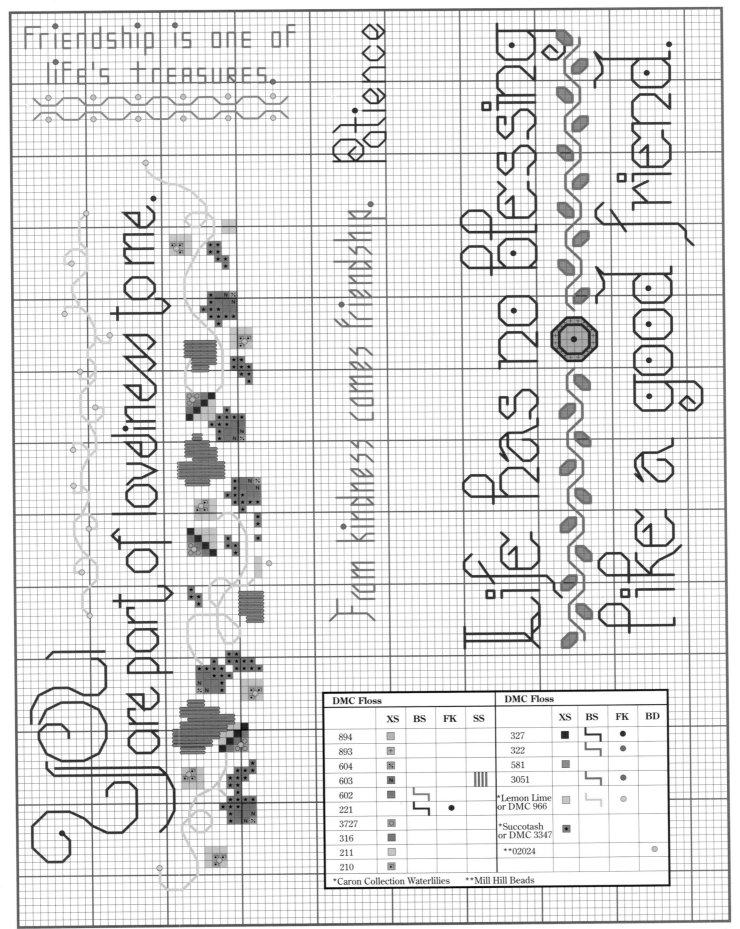

Friendship is one of life's treasures.

...are part of loveliness tome.

Patience

From kindness comes friendship.

...are part of loveliness lot.

Life has no blessing like a good friend.

DMC Floss					DMC Floss				
	XS	BS	FK	SS		XS	BS	FK	BD
894					327	■		●	
893	+				322			●	
604					581	■			
603	N			‖‖‖	3051	■		●	
602	■				*Lemon Lime or DMC 966			●	
221			●		*Succotash or DMC 3347	★			
3727	⊙				**02024				⊙
316	■								
211									
210									
*Caron Collection Waterlilies **Mill Hill Beads									

Friends Forever

Because I have been given much I too must give.

DMC Floss	XS	BS	FK	DMC Floss	XS	BS	FK	DMC Floss	XS	BS	FK
White	⊡			221		⌐		437	▢		
745	⊟			747	▢			436	▨		
445	▢			3325	▢			3827	s		
725	▢			824		⌐	●	420		⌐	
676	△			772	▢			840		⌐	●
3822	◎			368	+			844		⌐	●
3820	⊡	⌐		320	▢			898	■	⌐	●
782				504	⊠			3787	▨		
951	⊿	⌐	●	501	H	⌐		3072	▢		
3801	▢			3819	⊡			648	U		
350	N			3011		⌐	●	646	▢		
3608	▢			472	▢			3021		⌐	
3607	❋			471	Z			*Lemon Lime or DMC 368	★		
718	▢	⌐		469		⌐					
3803	E	⌐									

*Caron Collection Waterlilies

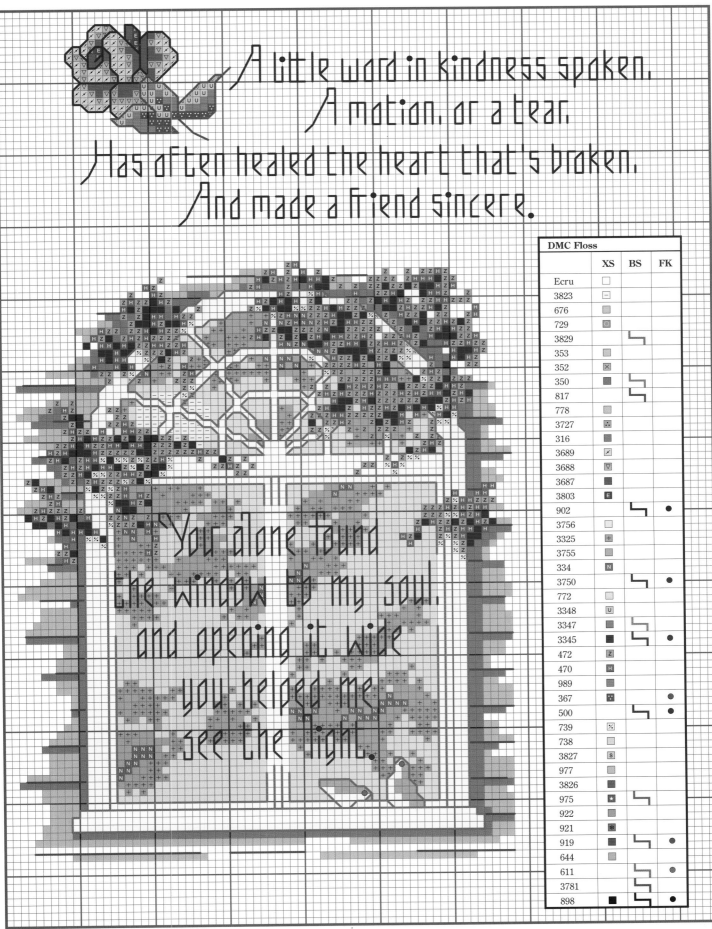

A little word in kindness spoken,
A motion, or a tear,
Has often healed the heart that's broken,
And made a friend sincere.

You alone found
the window to my soul,
and opening it wide
you helped me
see the light.

DMC Floss	XS	BS	FK
Ecru	□		
3823	–		
676			
729	◉		
3829		⌐	
353			
352	✕		
350		⌐	
817		⌐	
778			
3727	∴		
316			
3689	✎		
3688	▽		
3687			
3803	E		
902		⌐	●
3756			
3325	+		
3755			
334	N		
3750		⌐	●
772			
3348	U		
3347		⌐	
3345		⌐	●
472	Z		
470	H		
989			
367	⁛		●
500		⌐	●
739	✕		
738			
3827	S		
977			
3826			
975	✦	⌐	
922			
921	✳		
919		⌐	●
644			
611		⌐	●
3781		⌐	
898		⌐	●

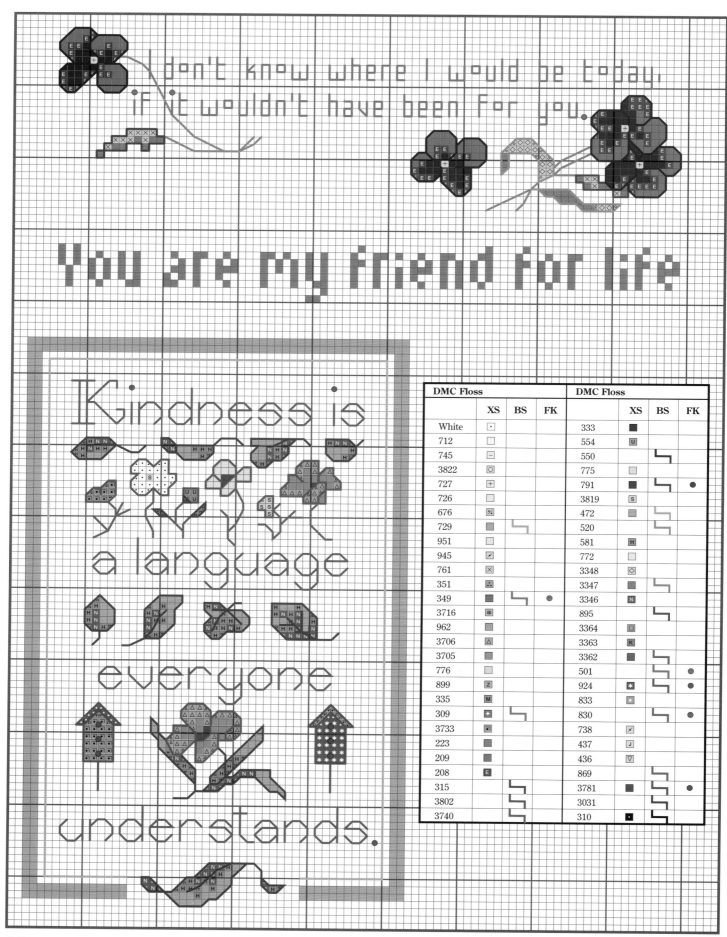

I don't know where I would be today, if it wouldn't have been for you.

You are my friend for life

Kindness is a language everyone understands.

DMC Floss				DMC Floss			
	XS	BS	FK		XS	BS	FK
White	·			333	■		
712	□			554	U		
745	−			550		⌐	
3822	⊙			775	□		
727	+			791	■	⌐	●
726	□			3819	S		
676	▨			472	■	⌐	
729	■	⌐		520		⌐	
951	□			581	H		
945	◪			772	□		
761	⊠			3348	◇		
351	▦			3347	■		
349	■	⌐	●	3346	N		
3716	✳			895		⌐	
962	■			3364	▢		
3706	△			3363	K		
3705	■			3362	■	⌐	
776	■			501		⌐	●
899	Z			924	✳	⌐	●
335	M			833	★		
309	✚	⌐		830		⌐	●
3733	▪			738	◩		
223	■			437	J		
209	■			436	▽		
208	E			869		⌐	
315		⌐		3781	■	⌐	●
3802		⌐		3031		⌐	
3740		⌐		310	▪	⌐	

Friendship

Best
Friends

Cherish
Laughter

Caring
Trust

You share
my dreams

11

I owe whatever
I was in life
To your hope
that would not
give me up,
To your love
that saw me
still as good.

SINCERE   THOUGHTFUL

To try to thank you
for being my friend
would require a lifetime.

Fun
Reliable
Ideal
Enjoy
Nice
Dear
Sweet

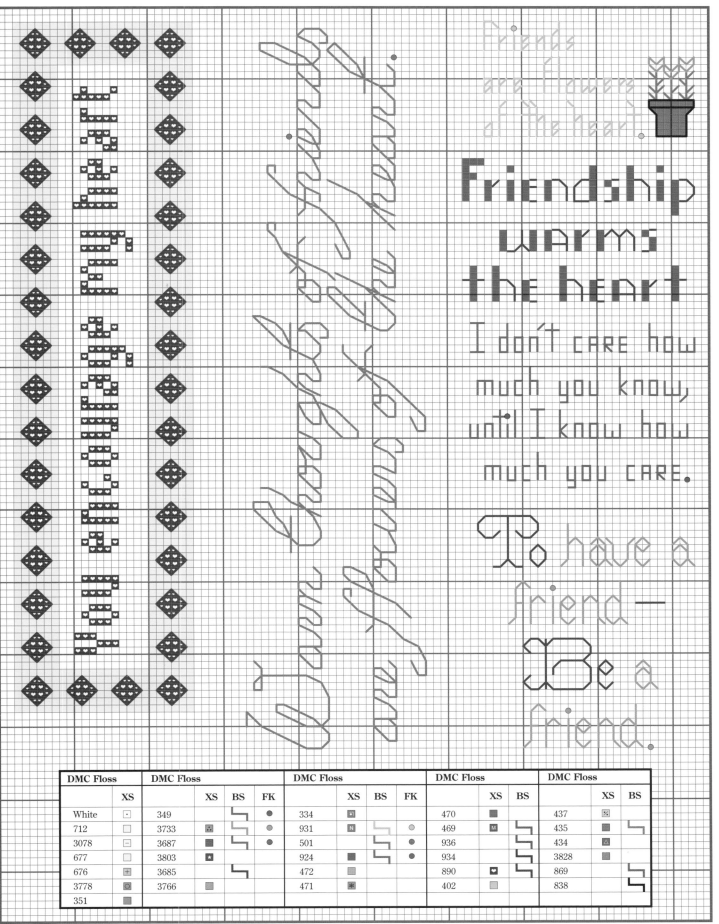

Friends are flowers of the heart.

Friendship warms the heart

I don't care how much you know, until I know how much you CARE.

To have a friend — Be a friend.

DMC Floss		DMC Floss				DMC Floss				DMC Floss			DMC Floss		
	XS		XS	BS	FK		XS	BS	FK		XS	BS		XS	BS
White	·	349		⌐	●	334	▣			470	▦		437	▨	
712	☐	3733	⁙	⌐	●	931	N	⌐	○	469	M	⌐	435	■	
3078	⊟	3687	■	⌐	●	501		⌐	●	936		⌐	434	△	
677	☐	3803	★			924	■	⌐	●	934		⌐	3828	■	
676	+	3685		⌐		472	▦			890	♥	⌐	869		⌐
3778	◎	3766	■			471	✳			402	▦		838		⌐
351	■														

Friendships
multiply joy and
divide grief

Some friends
wish you Happiness
one others wish you wealth
But I wish you the best
of all contentment
blessed with
Health.

The Beauty
of Friendship

Friends
are the flowers
in the garden
of life

Friends
are a gift
to treasure

Be my
Valentine

Friends
are a gift
to treasure

Friends are the flowers in the garden of life.

BEE MY HONEY

BEE MINE

The Beauty of Friendship

Forever
seemed too
short a time
for their
Friendship

Friendships
multiply our
blessings

Be my
friend

Good friends

I wish you happiness

and others wish you wealth

But I wish you contentment and the best

of all contentment blessed with health

DMC Floss				
	XS	BS	FK	BD
3731		⌐		
3740			●	
3756			○	
799	■	⌐	●	
798		⌐	●	
796		⌐	●	
561		⌐		
*40020				●
*Mill Hill Beads				

Heartfelt

To be confronted with our shadow reveals to us our Light.

It is not how much we have but how much we ENJOY that makes happiness.

It is by believing in roses that one brings them to bloom

The grass withers the flowers fade but the word of our God will stand forever.

Peace, Love and Joy to all who enter here.

I heard a bird sing In the dark of December A magical thing And sweet to remember.

The grass withers the flowers fade

but the word of our God will stand forever.

There is beauty all around.

It is by beleiving in roses that one brings them to bloom

DMC Floss		DMC Floss				DMC Floss			
	XS		XS	BS	FK		XS	BS	FK
3822		3350				501			
3820	N	3685				927			
729		315			●	3053			
3733	+	793				3052	E		
3731		823			●	3362			●
3354		502				420			

DMC Floss				DMC Floss				
	XS	BS	FK		XS	BS	FK	BD
712	☐			799	▣			
3078	☐			792	■			
677	⊟			791		⌐	●	
676	■			336	△			
729		⌐		823		⌐		
3820	▨			907	■			
945	■			472	⊠			
761	■			502	■			
351	■	⌐		738	◪			
3733	▨		●	436	H			
3350	■			976	■			
326		⌐	●	975		⌐	●	
3688	⊞			422				
3685	N	⌐	●	3774	◈			
3727	◉			3772		⌐		
316	E			869		⌐		
3726		⌐	●	839	■			
3803	✳	⌐		3781		⌐	●	
333		⌐	●	*62031				○
3325	■							
*Mill Hill Beads								

It is not
how much
we have
but
how much
we
ENJOY
that makes
happiness.

Sweetheart

life is
God!

You will always
be in my heart.

Dream with me

Heartfelt

I heard
a bird sing
In the dark
of December
A magical
thing
And sweet
to remember.

Wishing you the moon and stars.

May your joys be many, your sorrows few.

Make your own rainbows.

Memories of the Heart

May your wishes have wings to carry your dreams.

Smile.

It is the key that fits the lock
of everybody's heart.

A smile is a
hug from the heart.

your heart

Follow

DMC Floss				
	XS	**BS**	**FK**	**LS**
White	·			
Ecru	–		○	
3823				
744	⊠			
444				
725	◎			
677	+			
676				
783				
781			●	
951				
945				
605				
604	△		●	
603	E			
601			●	
3609	◈			
3608				
3607	Z		●	
3685				
211				
210				
3747				
341				
340	H			
3746			●	
3740				
828				
794	✳			
3807	⊡		●	
471				
470	N			
3808				
739	▢			
435				
434	M			
977				
420	S			
869	▣		●	
938				
801				
644				
642	★			
844			●	

Happiness

is always

an inside job.

Mother

Peace, Love and Joy to all who enter here.

A mother holds her

children's hands for a while.

but their hearts forever.

Sweet Violet Modesty

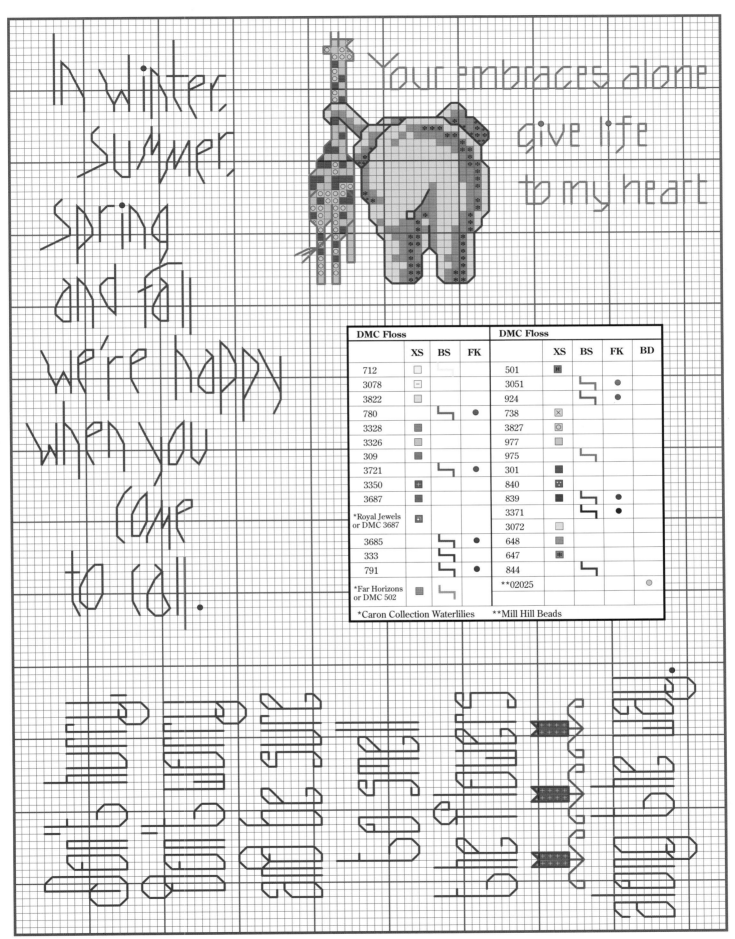

In Winter Summer spring and fall we're happy when you come to call.

Your embraces alone give life to my heart

DMC Floss				DMC Floss				
	XS	BS	FK		XS	BS	FK	BD
712	☐			501	H			
3078	−			3051		⌐	●	
3822	☐			924		⌐	●	
780		⌐	●	738	⊠			
3328	■			3827	◎			
3326	■			977	■			
309	■			975		⌐		
3721		⌐	●	301	■			
3350	+			840	⊡			
3687	■			839	■	⌐	●	
*Royal Jewels or DMC 3687	⊞			3371		⌐	●	
				3072	☐			
3685		⌐	●	648	■			
333		⌐		647	✳			
791		⌐	●	844		⌐		
*Far Horizons or DMC 502	■	⌐		**02025				◉
*Caron Collection Waterlilies				**Mill Hill Beads				

HOME IS WHERE
THE HEART IS

HEART and SOUL

the key

DMC Floss

	XS	BS	FK	SS	AE
Ecru	−				✳
677					
3822	+				
951					
945	◪				
3689				‖‖‖	
3688	◉				
3687	■				
3803	✦				
747					
3761	◉				
794	N				
3807			●		
807	■				
806	E				
3808					
3819					
472					
470	✶				
469	■				
524					
3363	▲				
3362	■				
422	✕				
869			●		

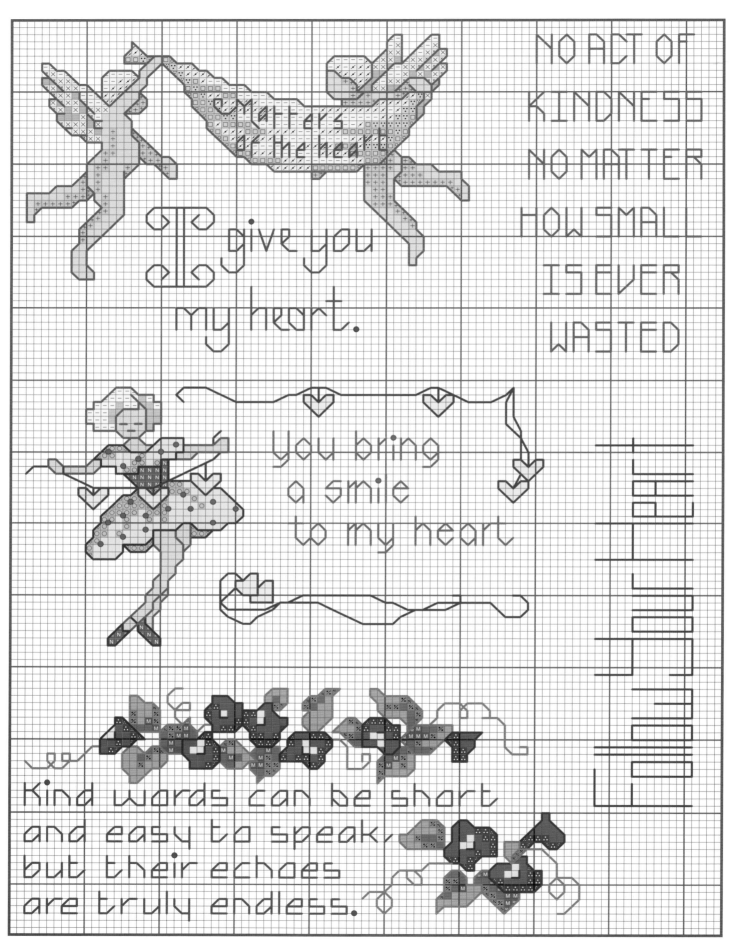

Matters of the heart

give you

my heart.

You bring
a smile
to my heart

Kind words can be short
and easy to speak,
but their echoes
are truly endless.

NO ACT OF
KINDNESS
NO MATTER
HOW SMAL
IS EVER
WASTED

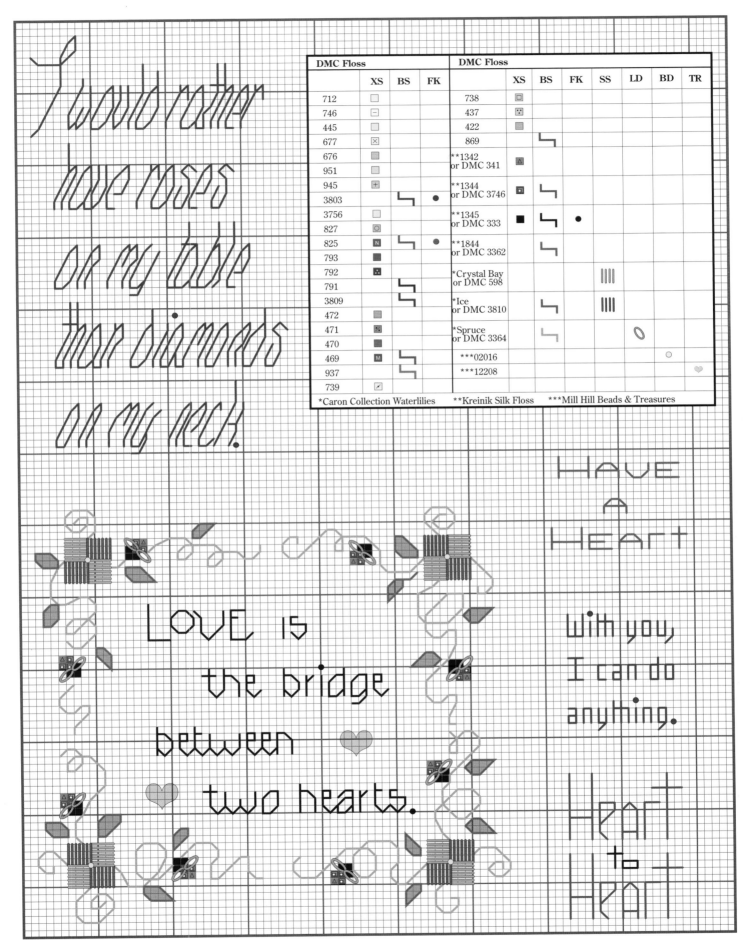

DMC Floss	XS	BS	FK
712	□		
746	−		
445	□		
677	⊠		
676	■		
951	□		
945	+		
3803		⌐	●
3756	□		
827	○		
825	N	⌐	●
793	■		
792	⊡		
791		⌐	
3809		⌐	
472	▦		
471	⊡		
470	■		
469	M	⌐	
937		⌐	
739	◹		

DMC Floss	XS	BS	FK	SS	LD	BD	TR
738	▫						
437	▦						
422	▦						
869		⌐					
**1342 or DMC 341	△						
**1344 or DMC 3746	⊡	⌐					
**1345 or DMC 333	■	⌐	●				
**1844 or DMC 3362		⌐					
*Crystal Bay or DMC 598				‖‖			
*Ice or DMC 3810		⌐		‖‖			
*Spruce or DMC 3364		⌐			∅		
***02016						○	
***12208							♥

*Caron Collection Waterlilies   **Kreinik Silk Floss   ***Mill Hill Beads & Treasures

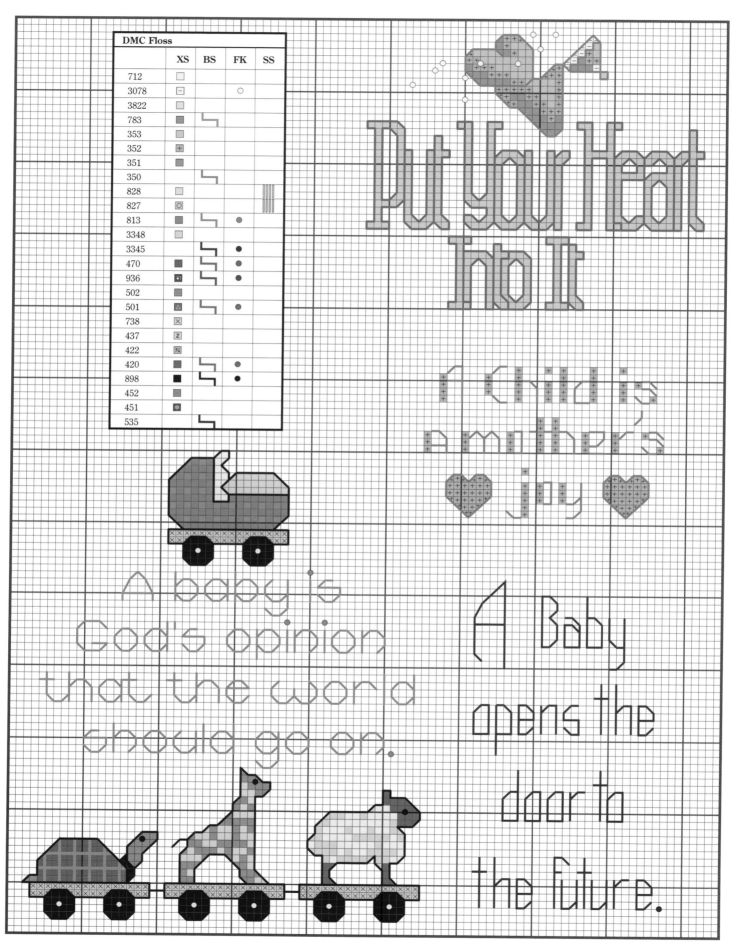

The only condition
for loving
is to love
without condition.

Two
Hearts
One
Soul

WARM

Devotion

TENDERNESS

May the Heavens
reward you each day
For the love
I can never repay.

are windows

your words

soft as a feather

Celebrations

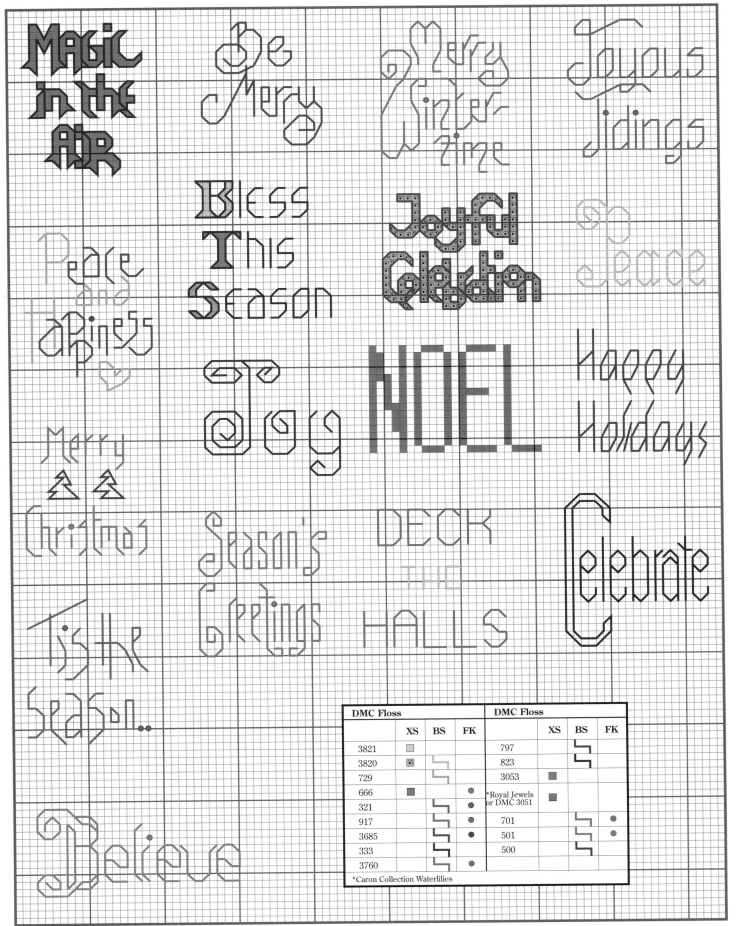

DMC Floss				DMC Floss			
	XS	BS	FK		XS	BS	FK
3821	▨			797		⌐	
3820	▣	⌐		823		⌐	
729		⌐		3053	▪		
666	▪		●	*Royal Jewels or DMC 3051	▪		
321		⌐	●				
917		⌐	●	701		⌐	●
3685		⌐	●	501		⌐	●
333		⌐	●	500		⌐	
3760		⌐	●				
*Caron Collection Waterlilies							

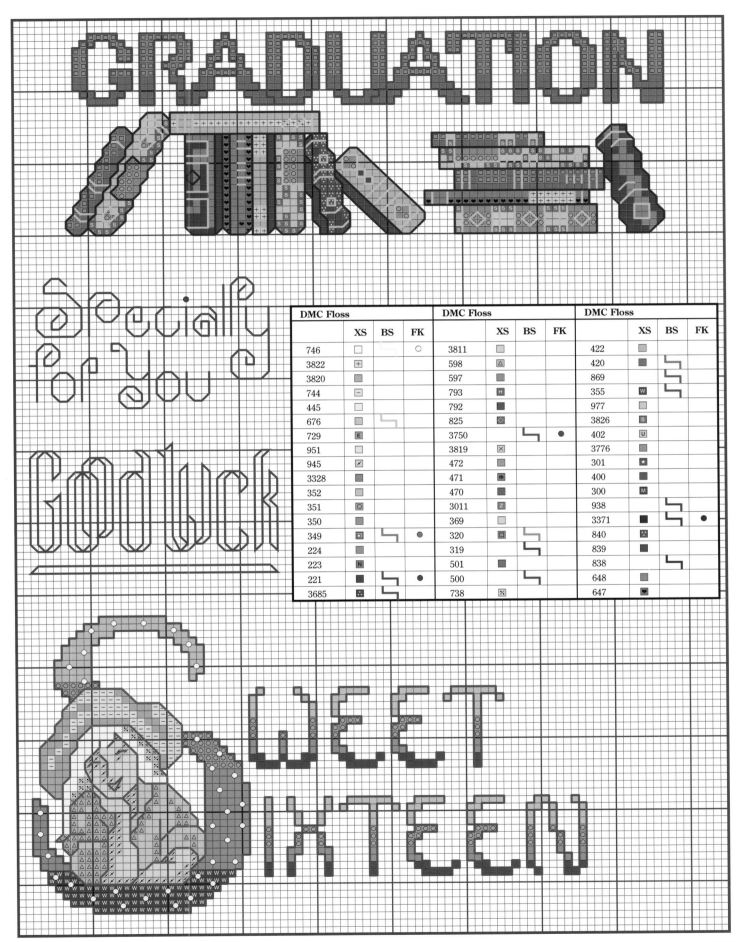

DMC Floss				DMC Floss				DMC Floss			
	XS	BS	FK		XS	BS	FK		XS	BS	FK
746	□		○	3811	▨			422	▨		
3822	+			598	△			420	▪	⌐	
3820	▨			597	▨			869		⌐	
744	−			793	H			355	W	⌐	
445	▨			792	▪			977	▨		
676	▨	⌐		825	◈			3826	S		
729	E			3750		⌐	●	402	U		
951	□			3819	⊠			3776	▨		
945	◪			472	▨			301	★		
3328	▨			471	✳			400	▪		
352	▨			470	▨			300	M		
351	◎			3011	Z			938		⌐	
350	▨			369	▨			3371	▪	⌐	●
349	▣	⌐	●	320	▣	⌐		840	▦		
224	▨			319		⌐		839	▪		
223	N			501	▪			838		⌐	
221	▪	⌐	●	500		⌐		648	▨		
3685	▨			738	▨			647	❤		

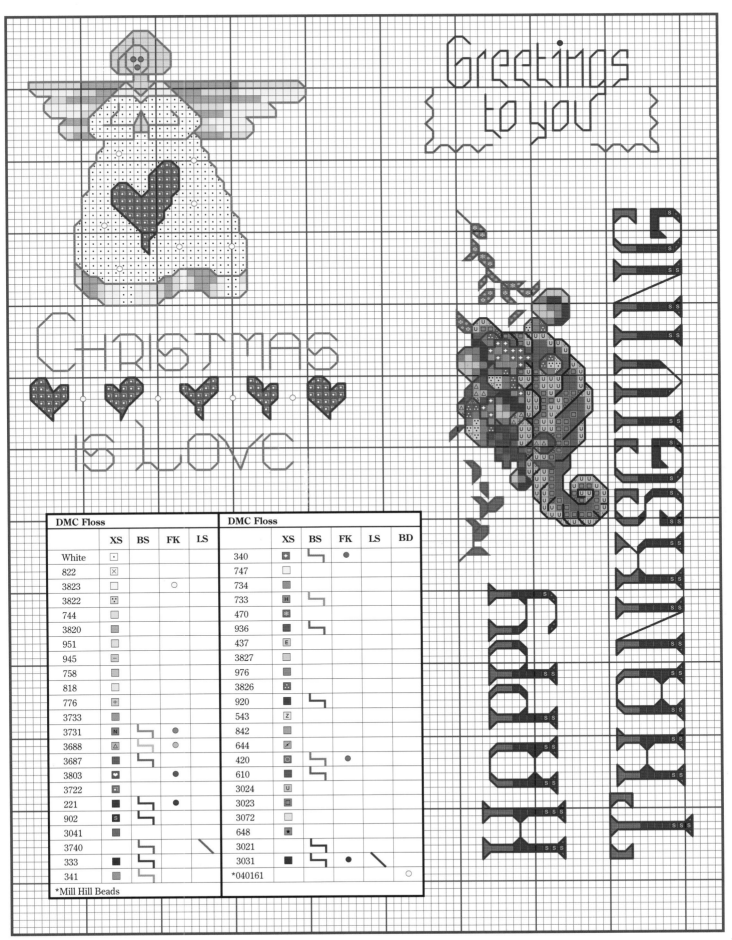

DMC Floss				
	XS	BS	FK	LS
White	·			
822	⊠			
3823	□		○	
3822	⊡			
744	□			
3820	■			
951	□			
945	−			
758	■			
818	□			
776	+			
3733	■			
3731	N	⌐	●	
3688	△	⌐	●	
3687	■	⌐		
3803	♥		●	
3722	◪			
221	■	⌐	●	
902	S	⌐		
3041	■			
3740		⌐		/
333	■	⌐		
341	■	⌐		
*Mill Hill Beads				

DMC Floss					
	XS	BS	FK	LS	BD
340	✛	⌐	●		
747	□				
734	■				
733	H	⌐			
470	✳				
936	■	⌐			
437	E				
3827	□				
976	■				
3826	⊡	⌐			
920	■	⌐			
543	Z				
842	■				
644	◪				
420	○	⌐	●		
610	■				
3024	U				
3023	▣				
3072	□				
648	★				
3021		⌐		/	
3031	■	⌐	●	/	
*040161					○

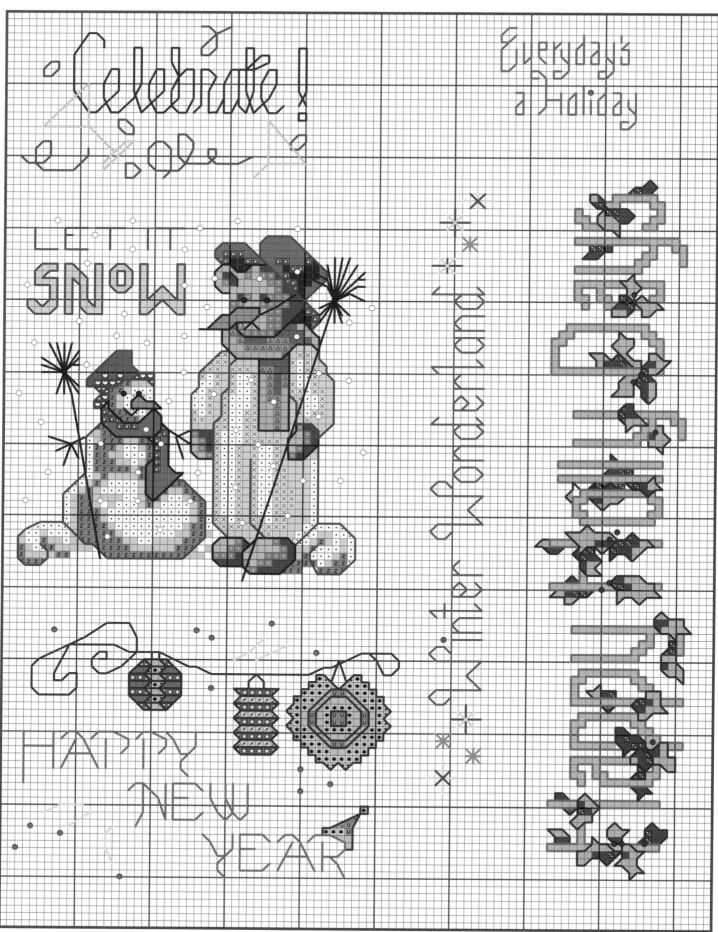

DMC Floss					DMC Floss					DMC Floss				DMC Floss					
	XS	BS	FK	LS		XS	BS	FK			XS	BS			XS	BS	FK	LS	BD
White	·		○		721	U				3756	⊠			644	▣	⌐			
712	▢			╱	352	▤				775	▤			420					
3822	⊿	⌐			351	△				518	E			402	◈				
676	▤				349	▣	⌐	●		3807		⌐		3776	⊞				
744	◎				209	▤				791		⌐		301	▣				
726	✳				208	⊡				807	▣			841	N				
725	S				333	■	⌐			806	♥	⌐		801		⌐	●	╱	
972	▤			⌐	3747	▤				368	▤			898	■	⌐	●		
783	⊞	⌐	●		341	Z	⌐			367	■	⌐		*00123					○
951	▤				3746	✦	⌐	●		500	⊠	⌐		*60367					●
*Mill Hill Beads																			

37

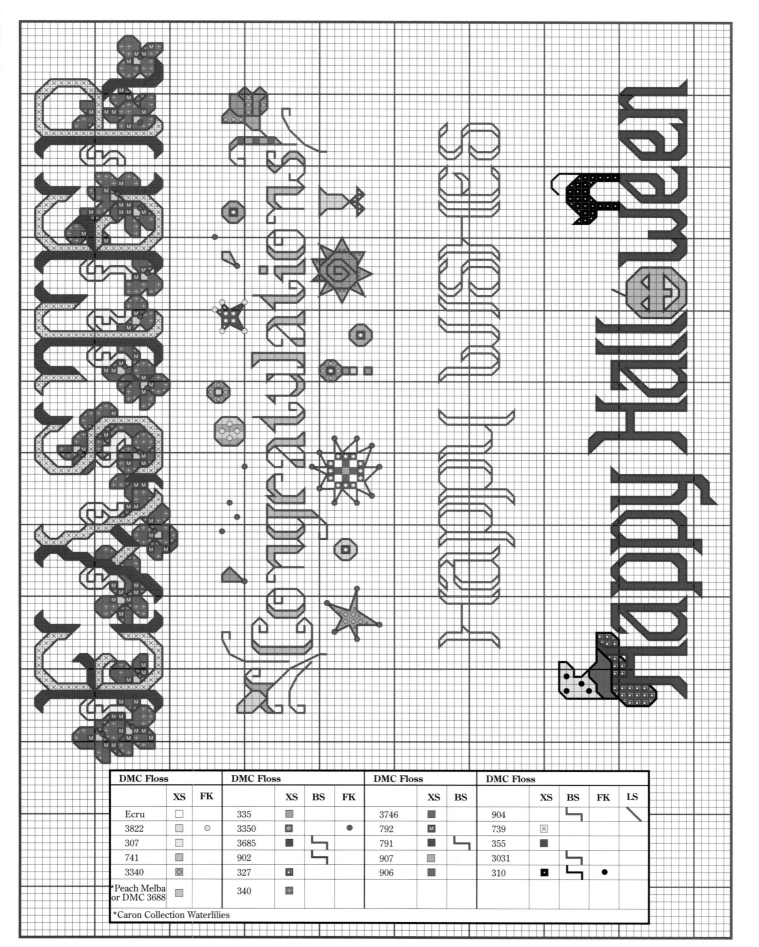

DMC Floss			DMC Floss				DMC Floss			DMC Floss				
	XS	FK		XS	BS	FK		XS	BS		XS	BS	FK	LS
Ecru	☐		335	■			3746	■		904		⌐		╱
3822	☐	◦	3350	✸		●	792	M		739	⊠			
307	☐		3685	■	⌐		791	■	⌐	355	■			
741	■		902	■	⌐		907	■		3031			⌐	
3340	◎		327	▣			906	■		310	▪	⌐	●	
*Peach Melba or DMC 3688	■		340	✛										
*Caron Collection Waterlilies														

DMC Floss	XS	BS	LS
Ecru	−	⌐	
677	◹		
676	△		
729	■	⌐	
726	+		
3820	N		\
722	■		
351	⊡		

DMC Floss	XS	BS	FK
3688	■		
3687	■	⌐	●
666	■		
321	◉	⌐	
815	W		
341	■		
340	E		
3746	■		

DMC Floss	XS	BS	FK
927	■		
3768	■	⌐	●
734	■		
733	★		
3364	×		
3363	■		
3362	H	⌐	
320	⊡		

DMC Floss	XS	BS	FK	BD
319	■	⌐	●	
739	□			
738	U			
437	□			
435	■			
869	⊡			
3031	■	⌐		
*00556				●

*Mill Hill Beads

Let's
Celebrate

Cheers

Here's
to you

Build
Long
Live

Let's
Party Time

The end
is the
Beginning

New
Beginnings

DMC Floss	XS	BS	FK
White	·		○
743	◎		
676			
352			
351			●
817			
815			●
604			
602			
210			
3740			
3761			
772			
3347			
703			
907			
3810			

Have your cake

and eat it, too.

WELCOME sweet FRIENDS

My IDEA of housework is to Sweep the room with a GLANCE

GIRL TALK

Angels gather here

Father

Mother

Sister

Brother

A mother's love

knows no end.

FAMILY MATTERS

God is the perfect parent

Some
people
came into our lives
and quickly go.
Some stay
for awhile
and leave
footprints
in our hearts
And we are
never the same

A friend is someone who reaches for your hand, but touches your heart.

Mother

Grandmothers are GREAT

Mother knows best

Enter with a happy heart.

DMC Floss				DMC Floss				DMC Floss				DMC Floss			DMC Floss			
	XS	BS	FK		XS	BS	FK		XS	BS	FK		XS	BS		XS	BS	FK
3078	☐		○	352	⊡			3727	▨			827	⊠		472	▨		
3822	▨		○	350	❋			316	E			798	■	⌐	471	N		
3820	▧		⌐	817			⌐	315	■	⌐		931	✚		470	■	⌐	●
782	■	⌐	●	225	◿			3609	◉		○	3811	▢		436	Z		
951	⊟			961	H		●	211	☐			807	K	⌐	869		⌐	
3824	✚			3326	⊠			209	M			3364	▣		838		⌐	
722	△		●	335	■	⌐	●	208	■	⌐	●							
353	▨			326	★	⌐	●											

Happy Home

HOME IS WHERE THE HEART IS

A perfect wife is one who helps her husband with the dishes.

It is admirable for a man to take his son fishing, but there is a special place in heaven for the father who takes his daughter shopping.

DMC Floss			
	XS	BS	FK
White	·		
Ecru	−	⌐	○
3078	□		
3822	⊠		
676	▦		
758	▦		
3778	◪		
776	▦		
3326	⊙		
335	E		
351	▦		
350	✳		
*Prairie Fire or DMC 350	S		
3705	⋰	⌐	
3350	■		
3803	H	⌐	●
210	▦		
3041	Z		
3740		⌐	
775	△		
334		⌐	
792			●
3807	▽	⌐	●
747	□		
3766	▣		
3761	+		
518	▦		●
3811	▦		
597	K		
3810		⌐	
3809	■		
959	▦		
772	▦		
704	▣		
3819	▦		
471	▦		
3013	⊠		
976	N	⌐	
402	▦		
3776	▦		
3777		⌐	●
422	▦		
420	▦		
400	▨		
3830	■		
433	★		
3031		⌐	●
648	▦		
647	U		
646	♥		
3021		⌐	
*Caron Collection Waterlilies			

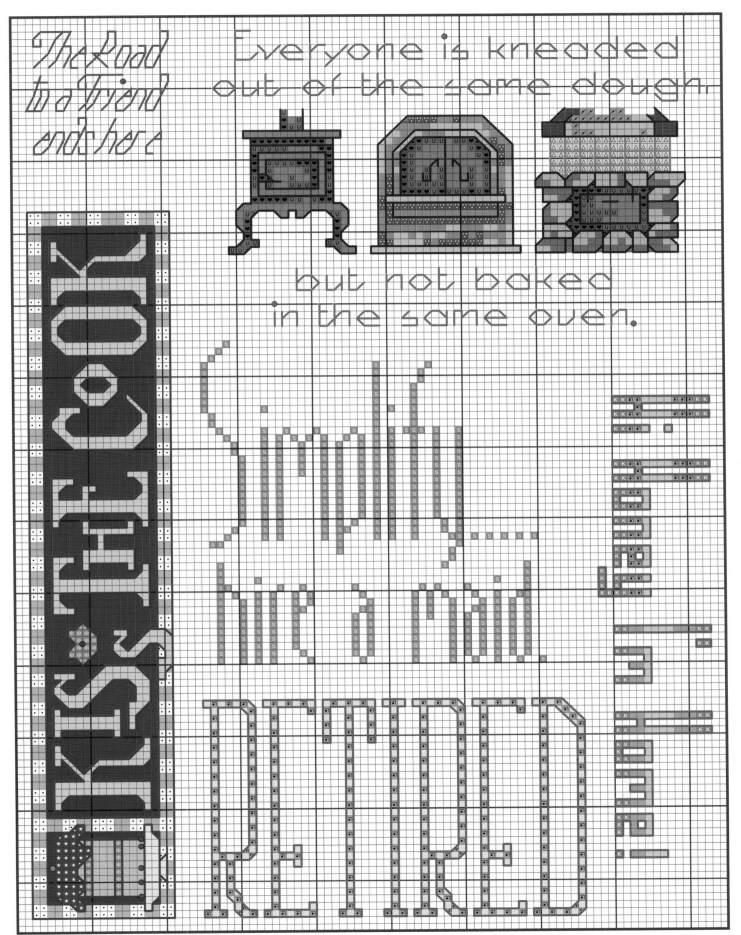

The Road to a friend ends here

Everyone is kneaded out of the same dough, but not baked in the same oven.

KISS THE COOK

RETIRED

47

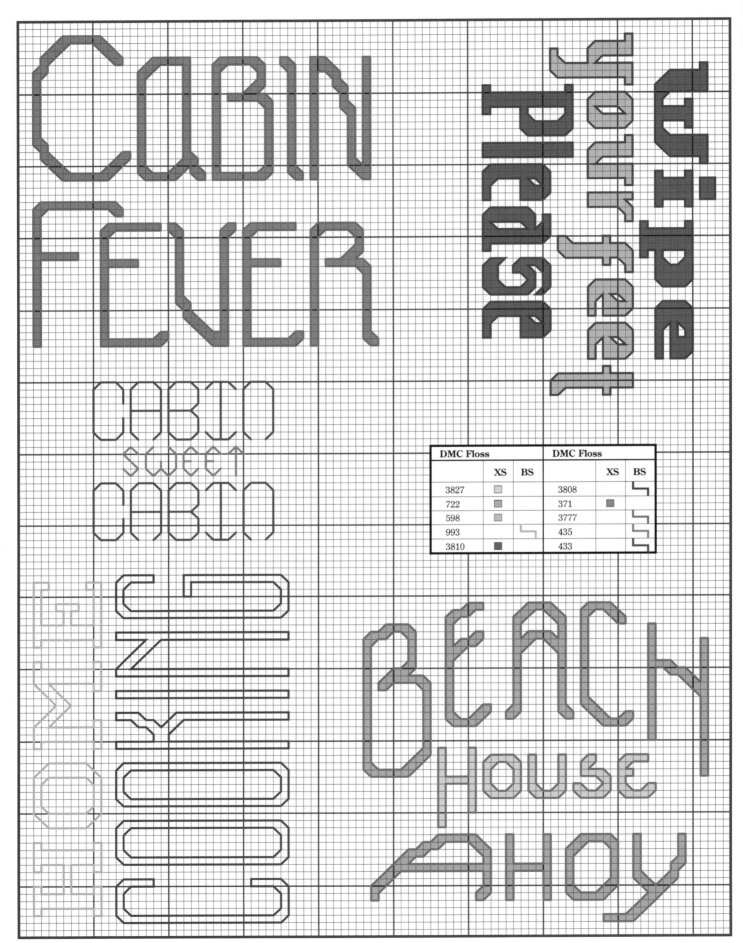

DMC Floss			DMC Floss		
	XS	BS		XS	BS
3827	▨		3808		⌐
722	▨		371	▪	
598	▨		3777		⌐
993		⌐	435		⌐
3810	▪		433		⌐

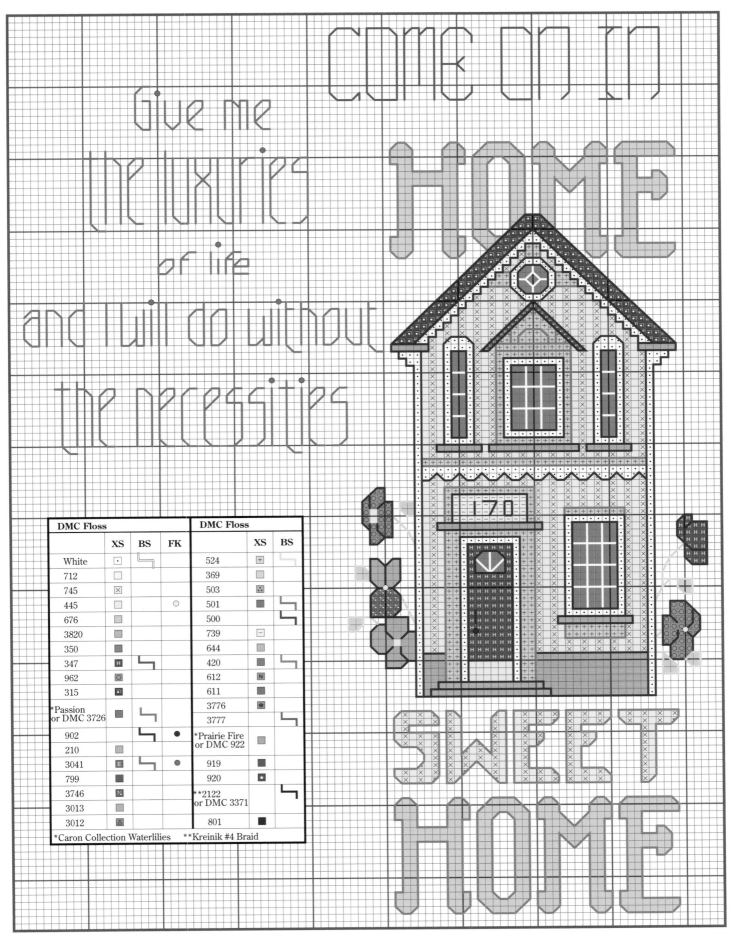

Come on in

Give me
the luxuries
of life
and I will do without
the necessities

HOME

SWEET
HOME

DMC Floss	XS	BS	FK	DMC Floss	XS	BS
White	·			524	+	
712				369		
745	⊠			503		
445			○	501		
676				500		
3820				739	−	
350				644		
347	H			420		
962	◎			612	N	
315	◪			611		
*Passion or DMC 3726				3776	✳	
				3777		
902			●	*Prairie Fire or DMC 922		
210				919		
3041	E		●	920	★	
799				**2122 or DMC 3371		
3746	✖			801		
3013						
3012	△					

*Caron Collection Waterlilies   **Kreinik #4 Braid

If you love something set it free.
If it returns, it's yours.
If it does not, it never was.

I LOVE MY DAD

HERE'S TO YOU DAD

WORLD'S GREATEST FATHER

DAD

DMC Floss							
	XS	BS	FK	LS	SS	LD	BD
Ecru	⊟			╱	‖‖‖		
745	▢						
726	◎						
783	▣						
945	▨						
722	⁙						
921	N						
349	✳	⌐					
962	▨						
326	▨	⌐	●				
3722	◼						
221	◼	⌐					
315	◪	⌐	●				
3755	▨	╱					
334	▨	⌐					
3807	E						
791		⌐					
3819	△						
3348	▨						
368	⊞						
320	▨						
367	✦	⌐				〇	
501		⌐					
3809		⌐					
3024	▢						
422	⊠			╱			
420	◼	⌐	●				
610		⌐	●				
3031		⌐					
*65270							●
*Mill Hill Beads							

Friend

Enjoy the Moment

Forget me not

Children aren't happy with nothing to ignore. And that's what parents were created for.

Families are Forever

Count Me Forever

Aunt

Uncle

Grandfathers are GREAT

Father

knows BEST

Many hands make light work.

I only know my mother's love which gives all and asks nothing.

Little girls are precious gifts, wrapped in love serene. Their dresses tied with sashes, and futures tied with dreams.

DMC Floss	XS	BS	FK	SS
712	□			‖‖‖‖
727	□			
725	−			
677	⊠			
729		⌐		
3820	△			
783	■		●	
782		⌐		
951	□			
3341	+			
352	■			
351	⊙			
350	■			

DMC Floss	XS	BS	FK	LD
349	■			
347	⊡	⌐		
3713	⊿			
760	◎			
3328	E			
3609	Z			
961	■			
3801	✳		●	
304		⌐	●	◯
3721		⌐		
3803		⌐		
209	■			
327			●	

DMC Floss	XS	BS	FK
3041	⊡		
3740		⌐	
826	N		
824		⌐	
3750		⌐	●
598	■		
3810	■		
3808		⌐	
3819	▢		
472	■		
471	H	⌐	
470	■	⌐	
935		⌐	●

DMC Floss	XS	BS	FK	LD
3348	▨			
3347		⌐		
3346		⌐		◯
966	■			
368	⊡	⌐		
367		⌐		
3364	U			
3815	■	⌐	●	
561	M			
500		⌐	●	
921	✶	⌐	●	
919		⌐	●	
869			●	

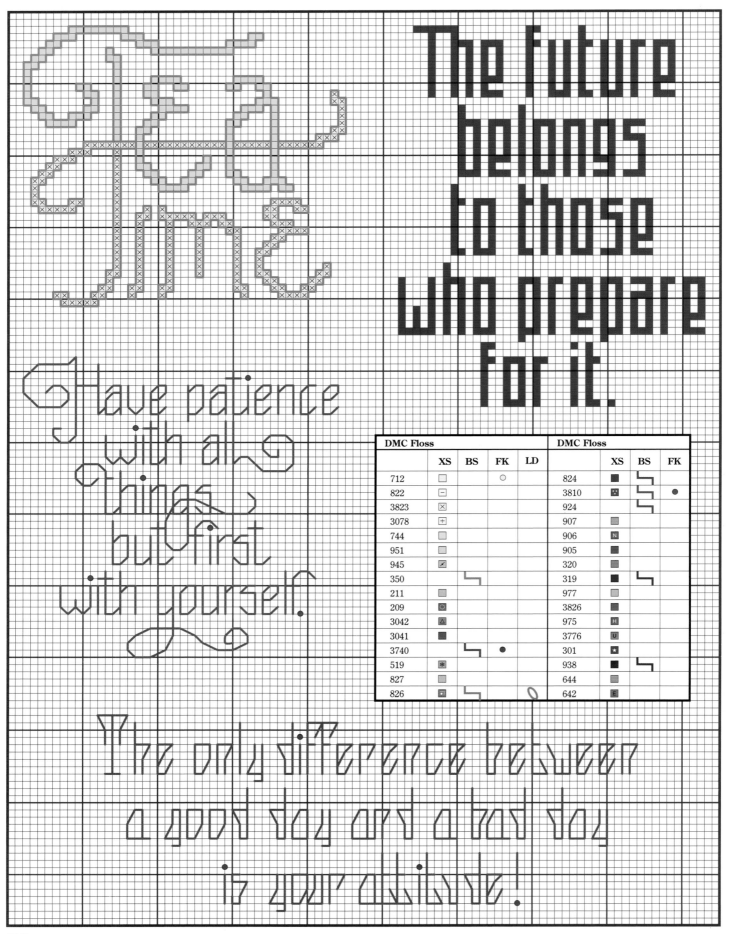

The future belongs to those who prepare for it.

Have patience with all things but first with yourself.

The only difference between a good day and a bad day is your attitude!

DMC Floss						DMC Floss			
	XS	BS	FK	LD			XS	BS	FK
712	□		○			824	■	⌐	
822	−					3810	▣	⌐	●
3823	⊠					924		⌐	
3078	+					907	▨		
744	□					906	N		
951	□					905	■		
945	▨					320	▨		
350		⌐				319	■	⌐	
211	▨					977	▨		
209	◉					3826	■		
3042	▲					975	H		
3041	■					3776	U		
3740		⌐	●			301	✦		
519	✳					938	■	⌐	
827	□					644	▨		
826	▣	⌐		◯		642	E		

We make a living
by what we get—

we make a life
by what we give.

HUGS and KISSES

The Most
important
THINGS
i·n l·i·f·e
aren't
THINGS

Pickle

Up!

Count On
Family

Busy
Hands
Happy
Hearts

L · I · F · E
is meant
to be spent
not to be saved

Life is uncertain
Eat dessert first

A warm smile
is the language
of kindness.

WISDOM

SET GOALS

I'm here
for you

DMC Floss				DMC Floss			
	XS	BS	FK		XS	BS	FK
White	·			930	★	⌐	
712	□			924	▦	⌐	
3823	⊟			993	■		●
3820	▨			502	▨		
783	⊡	⌐	●	910		⌐	●
350	■	⌐	●	977	▣		
775	+			976	▨		
3325	▨			420		⌐	
828	✕			3776	U		
827	◎			400	■		
813	E			840	■		
826		⌐	●	839	M		
3761		⌐	○	838		⌐	
3765	■	⌐		*001C or DMC 317		⌐	
931	▨						
*Kreinik Cord							

It is more
blessed
to give
than receive

We can't direct
the wind,

but we can

adjust

our sails.

If you want to be happy, be.

Babies come into this world
holding joy in their hands.

And when they open those small fingers,
The whole world's supply is replenished again.

The tragedy of life is not

that it ends so soon.

but that we wait

so long to begin it.

DMC Floss	XS	BS	FK	SS
White	·			
712	□			
744	=			
676	▦	(BS)		
729		(BS)		
3821	⊠			
783	▪		•	||||
351	▪		•	
350	⊞			
817		(BS)		
3727				

DMC Floss	XS	BS	FK	SS
*Rose Blush or DMC 316	▪			
315		(BS)		
3761	□	(BS)		
519	⊙			||||
518	▪			
3760	▫			
322	✳			
311	■	(BS)	•	
3053	▪	(BS)		

DMC Floss	XS	BS	FK
3011		(BS)	•
471	E		
581		(BS)	
520		(BS)	
*Evergreen or DMC 501	N		
561		(BS)	•
3809	■		
834	▪		
833			

DMC Floss	XS	BS	FK	BD
831		(BS)		
3827	△			
437	U			
3828	▪			
420	%			
869		(BS)	•	
839		(BS)	•	
648	▪			
**02001				○

*Caron Collection Waterlilies   **Mill Hill Beads

Good deeds
live long

Good deeds
never go
unrewarded

Candy
solves
everything

A man never stands as tall
as when he kneels to help a child.

I will be glad today

for the clouds or the rainbows

Smooth as our good meaning

Both are meant for my good

And without both, neither has meaning

DMC Floss					DMC Floss				
	XS	BS	FK	ES		XS	BS	FK	ES
712	□				794	■			
746	−				793				✳
677	✓				3807		⌐	●	
3822	□				792	■	⌐	●	
3821	▣				930		⌐	●	
726		⌐			3364	■			
3046	×				3363		⌐		
3045	■				472	⊡			
3774	□				906	■			
950	+				368	▧			
3341		⌐			320	■			✳
352	□				367	E	⌐	●	
351	◎				738	◇			
321	■	⌐			977	□			
902		⌐	●		3826	■			
3830	■	⌐			975	N			
209		⌐			869	✳	⌐		
3743	□				612				
3042	⠿			✳	611	H	⌐		
3041	■				632		⌐		
800	□				3031		⌐		
809	△								

Dream Learn Share Believe

Stop and smell the roses

Faith, Hope, Love

The manner of giving is worth more than the gift.

There are things we see for the first time... again and again.

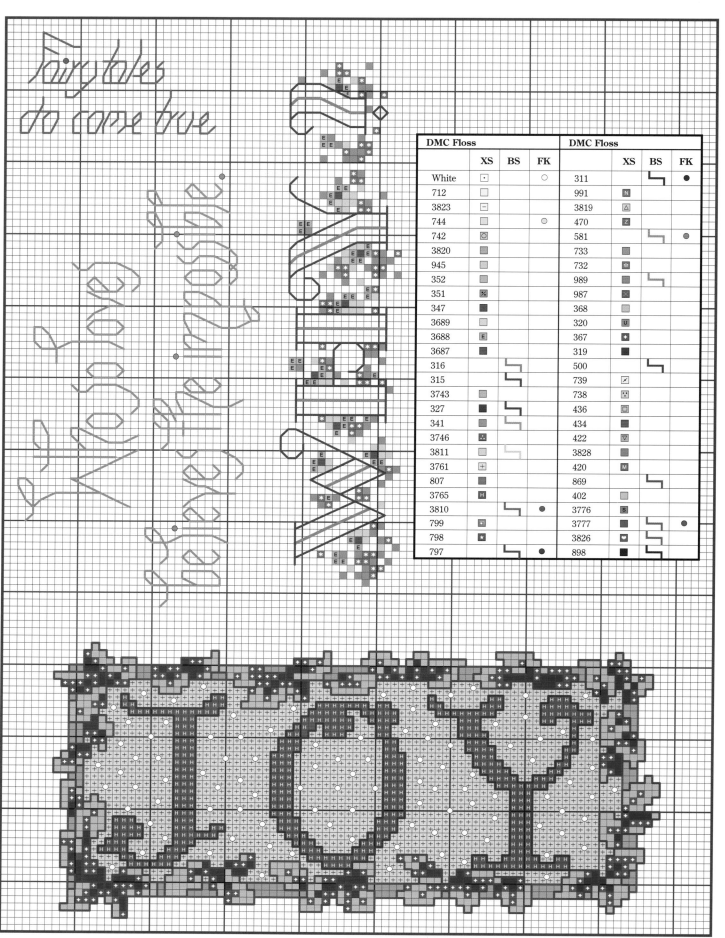

DMC Floss				DMC Floss			
	XS	BS	FK		XS	BS	FK
White	·		○	311		⌐	●
712	☐			991	N		
3823	⊟			3819	△		
744	☐		○	470	Z		
742	◎			581		⌐	●
3820	▣			733	▣		
945	▣			732	✳		
352	▣			989	✕		
351	⁒			987			
347	■			368	☐		
3689	☐			320	U		
3688	E			367	✦		
3687	▣			319	■		
316		⌐		500		⌐	
315		⌐		739	▱		
3743	▣			738	⬚		
327	■	⌐		436	⬚		
341	▣	⌐		434	■		
3746	⁙			422	▽		
3811	☐	⌐		3828	▣		
3761	⊞			420	M		
807	▣			869		⌐	
3765	H			402	▣		
3810		⌐	●	3776	S		
799	▣			3777	■	⌐	●
798	★			3826	♥		
797		⌐	●	898	■	⌐	

64

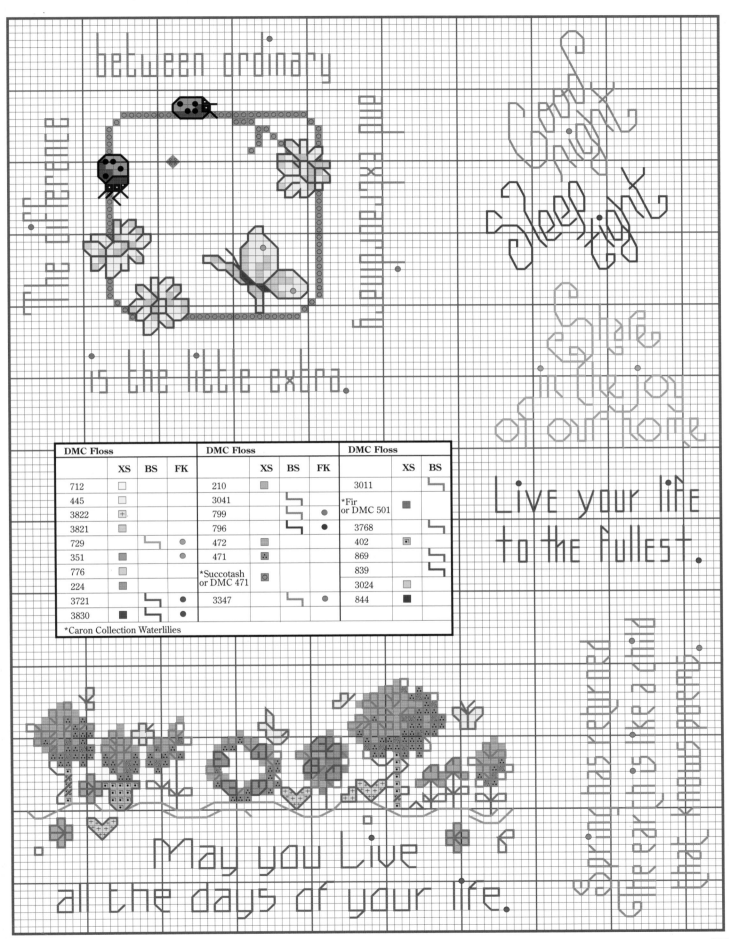

between ordinary

The difference

and extraordinary

is the little extra.

Good night
Sleep tight

Share
in the joy
of our home

Live your life
to the fullest

DMC Floss				DMC Floss				DMC Floss		
	XS	BS	FK		XS	BS	FK		XS	BS
712	☐			210	◪			3011		⌐
445	☐			3041		⌐		*Fir or DMC 501	◼	
3822	⊞			799		⌐	●	3768		⌐
3821	◻			796		⌐	●	402	▣	
729		⌐	●	472	◪			869		⌐
351	◼		●	471	▦			839		⌐
776	◻			*Succotash or DMC 471	◉			3024	◻	
224	◼							844	◼	
3721		⌐	●	3347		⌐	●			
3830	◼	⌐	●							

*Caron Collection Waterlilies

Spring has returned.
The earth is like a child
that knows poems.

May you Live
all the days of your life.

BELIEVE IN YOURSELF

Smile happily ever after

The best way
to pay for a lovely moment
is to enjoy it.

I tell you my dreams,
and while you are
listening to me,
I see them come true.

Life-Live it!

DMC Floss	XS	BS	FK	DMC Floss	XS	BS	FK
White	·			3013	▦		
Ecru			○	3012	▣		
3821	+			3011		⌐	
676	▦			3819	▦		
680	▦			581	E		
782	⁙			472	X		
950	▦			471	S		
352	◎			3362		⌐	●
351		⌐	●	367	▦		
3705	▦			911		⌐	●
666	▨	⌐	●	3345	◪		
816	▦	⌐	●	833	▦		
210	−			832	✳		
208		⌐		436	▦		
553	H			435	▦		
550	▦	⌐		434	★		
3743	▦			869		⌐	●
3042	△			841	▦		
3041	▦			648	Z		
3740		⌐		3371		⌐	●
3746	▦	⌐		310	▪	⌐	
3807	N	⌐	●				

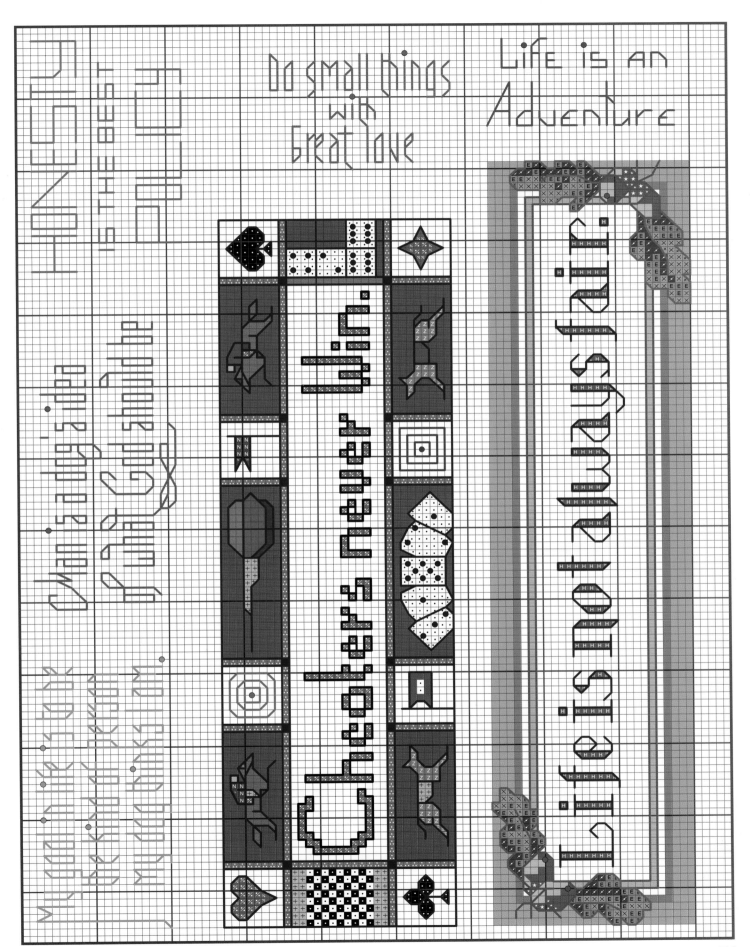

Do small things
with
Great love

Life is an
Adventure

Cheaters never win.

Life is not always fair.

Never give up!

The voyage of discovery is not in seeking new landscapes but in having new eyes.

in season at all times

Just do it

Success

GLORY

I'll always be there for you.

love is a fruit and within the reach of every hand.

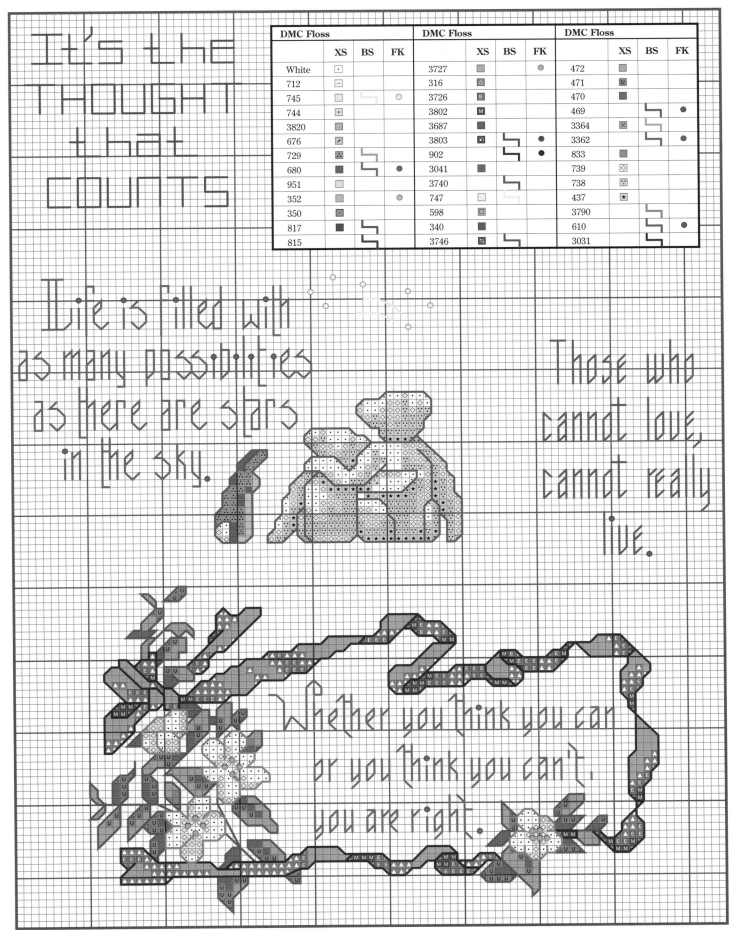

DMC Floss	XS	BS	FK	DMC Floss	XS	BS	FK	DMC Floss	XS	BS	FK
White	·			3727			●	472			
712	−			316				471	U		
745			○	3726	E			470			
744	+			3802	M			469		⌐	●
3820				3687				3364	⊠		
676	◹			3803	◪	⌐	●	3362		⌐	●
729	⠿	⌐		902		⌐	●	833			
680		⌐	●	3041				739	◇		
951				3740		⌐		738	⠅		
352			●	747				437	★		
350	◉			598	▢			3790		⌐	
817		⌐		340				610		⌐	●
815		⌐		3746	⊠	⌐		3031			

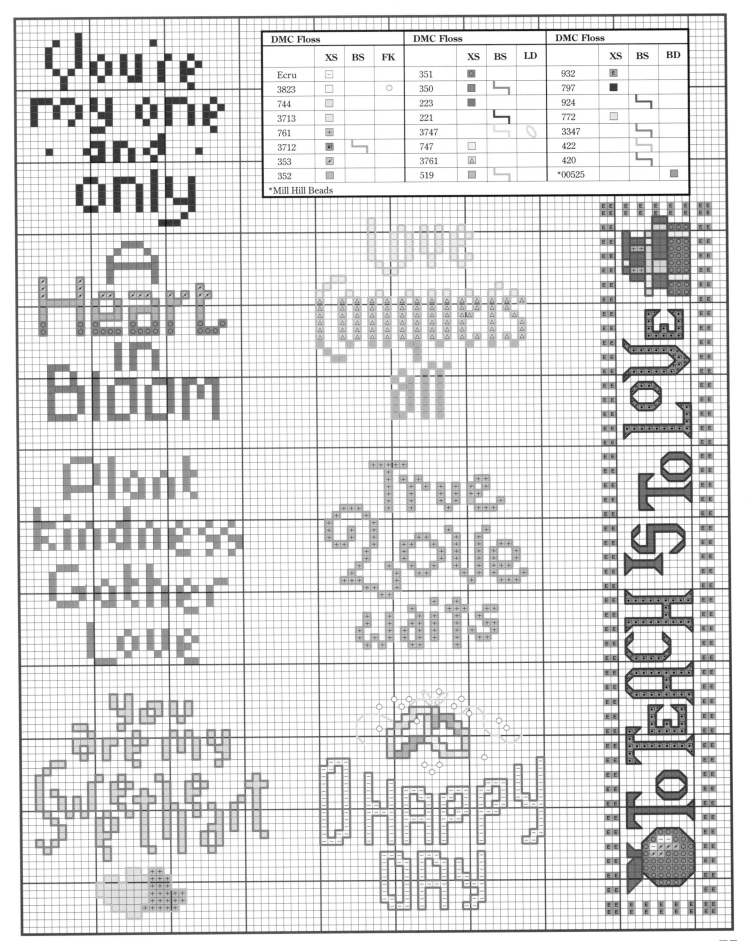

DMC Floss	XS	BS	FK	DMC Floss	XS	BS	LD	DMC Floss	XS	BS	BD
Ecru	−			351	◎			932	E		
3823	□		○	350	■	⌐		797	■		
744	▨			223	■			924		⌐	
3713	□			221		⌐		772	▨		
761	+			3747			○	3347		⌐	
3712	▣	⌐		747	□			422			
353	▨	⌐		3761	△			420		⌐	
352	▨			519	▨	⌐		*00525			▨
*Mill Hill Beads											

I know what LOVE is
it is because of

you

LOVE

is the source of

LIFE

For time
and all
ETERNITY

BLISS

I

LOVE

YOU

Love of my life.

from this day forward

Our hands,
Our hearts,
Our souls—
Perfect fits—

...and two shall
be as one...

Happy
Anniversary

BE YOURSELF

ON THIS
DAY
I THEE
WED

Bride

Groom

BEE MY

HONEY

What I Love
most at home
is near at hand

Boy

Girl

The following text is embroidered within the chart image:

Love is a giving thing

Love listens

I know love, because I know you

The following DMC Floss legend appears as a table:

DMC Floss	XS	BS	FK	DMC Floss	XS	BS	FK
White	·			315	G		
Ecru	−		○	3802			
746				902			
745	×			3761			
3821	◇			813			
725				312			
676	U			927			
783			●	3768			
950				924	R		●
761			○	3819			
760				732			
3712				772			
3328				989	K		
353	+			987			
347			●	3052			●
3801	E			3051			
819				472			
3326	%			471	N		
3731				470			
3354	S		○	3348			
3350				3347	W		
815				3345			
3689				504	▽		
3688	○			502			
3687	Z			368	J		
3803	M		●	319			●
3685				422			
3722	H			3828			
221	★			420			
778	△			869			
3727				975			
316				610			
3726			●	310	■		

DMC Floss				DMC Floss			
	XS	BS	FK		XS	BS	FK
745				341			
744	+			340			
727				3819			
3821				581	N		●
781			●	734	E		
3824	◎			733			
3328				732	★		
3713				3364	△		
3716				3012			
351				3011			
350				3051			
3705				472			
3354				471			
498			●	470			
221				469	H		
209				989			
3041				987			
915			●	420			
550							

Marriage –

Joy
• is the start of it
Sharing
• is a part of it
Love
• is the heart of it

I will love you and
Forever

My love...

Love is the reason

My heart

Belongs to you

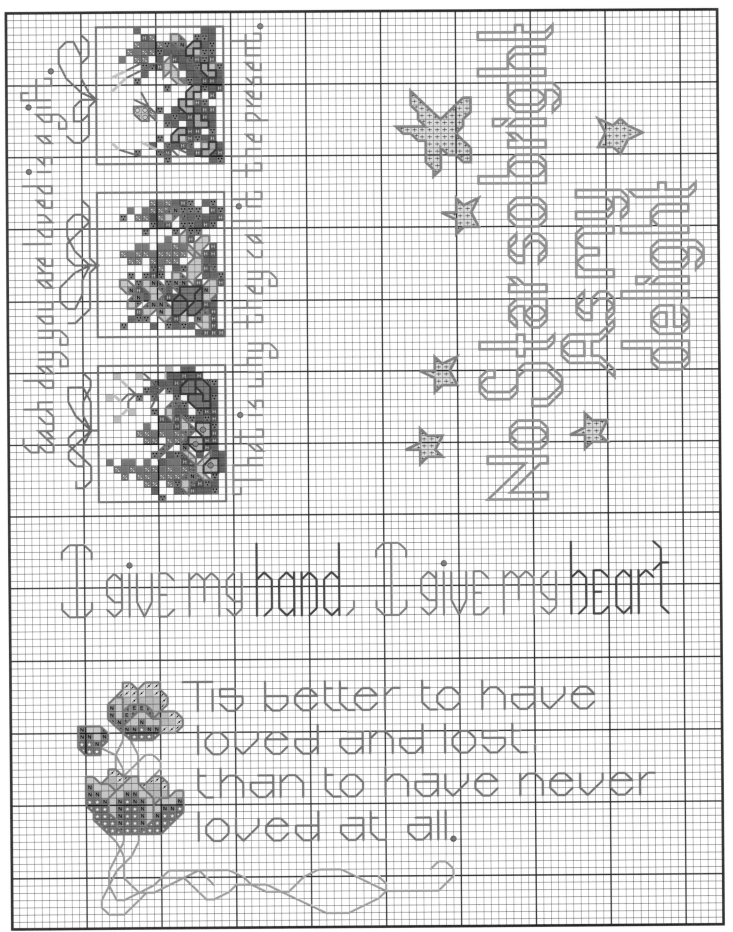

Each day you are loved a gift.

This is my gift — the present.

tis nice to be a star so bright

Nov. star light

I give my hand, I give my heart

Tis better to have
loved and lost
than to have never
loved at all.

DMC Floss			DMC Floss				DMC Floss		
	XS	BS		XS	BS	FK		XS	BS
Ecru	⊟		349	■	⌐	●	3347	M	
745	☐		225	◈			3819	☐	
744	⊞		224	■			472	⅗	
727	⊠		223	E			734	■	
725	☐		3721				937		⌐
3821	⠶		3802		⌐	●	3362		⌐
676	◉		818	☐			501		
729		⌐	776	U			738	▣	
783	■		816		⌐	●	420		⌐
780	■		3041	■			435	■	
951	☐		327	■			3033	☐	
945	◪		550		⌐	●	3782	N	
3779	△		798	■			3032	■	
353	☐		312		⌐	●	3790		⌐
352	S		820		⌐		801		⌐
351		⌐	3348	☐					

Baby's Sleeping

LOVE MAKES THE WORD GO ROUND

for giving.   for sharing.

Life is for joy.

and for laughter.

You are loved

A heart full of love.

Whoever has a heart full of love always has something to give.

but mostly – it's for Love.

Give a child two things Roots and Wings

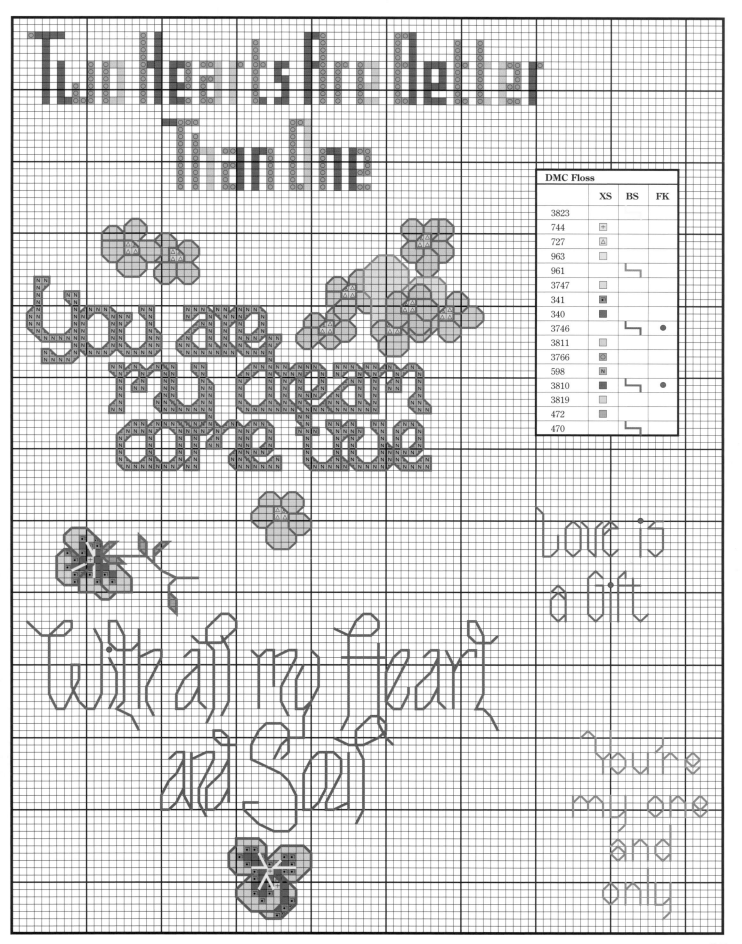

DMC Floss			
	XS	BS	FK
3823			
744	⊞		
727	△		
963	▢		
961		⌐	
3747	▢		
341	▣		
340	◼		
3746		⌐	●
3811	▢		
3766	◉		
598	N		
3810	◼	⌐	●
3819	▢		
472	◼		
470		⌐	

All creatures great and small,
the Lord God loves them all.

To love and be loved is to feel
the sun from both sides

PUPPY LOVE   You're the Cats Meow

dog   ANIMAL Lover

Love Me,
love My cat.

DMC Floss					DMC Floss			
	XS	BS	FK	LS		XS	BS	FK
White	·			/	3803	E	⌐	●
712	▢				3685		⌐	
745	✕				3768		⌐	●
743	▢				3011		⌐	●
677	−				402	▢		
676	◎				422	▨		
783	▨	⌐			869		⌐	●
350		⌐	●		738	▢		
349	▪				436	U		
817		⌐	●		435	▪		
3713	▢				434	▨		
3716	▨				433	▪		
962	▪				3777		⌐	
223	▣				356	◪		
3689	+		○		3830	✳	⌐	●
3688	△		○		839	♥	⌐	●
3687	▪				535	▪	⌐	

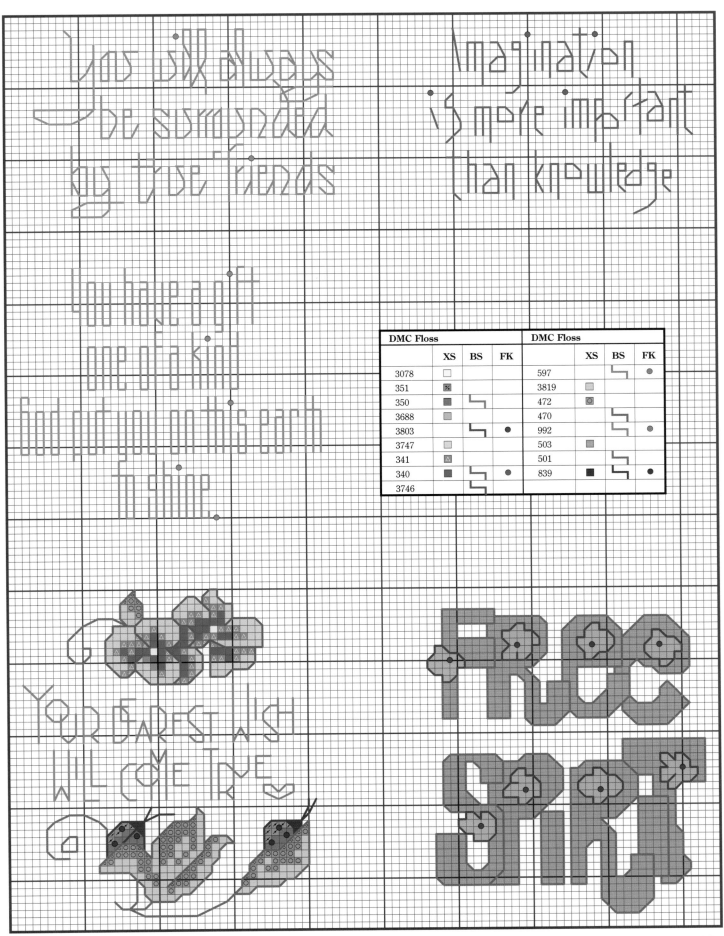

DMC Floss				DMC Floss			
	XS	BS	FK		XS	BS	FK
3078	☐			597		⌐	●
351	▨			3819	☐		
350	■	⌐		472	◉		
3688	■			470		⌐	
3803		⌐	●	992		⌐	●
3747	☐			503	■		
341	△			501		⌐	
340	■	⌐	●	839	■	⌐	●
3746		⌐					

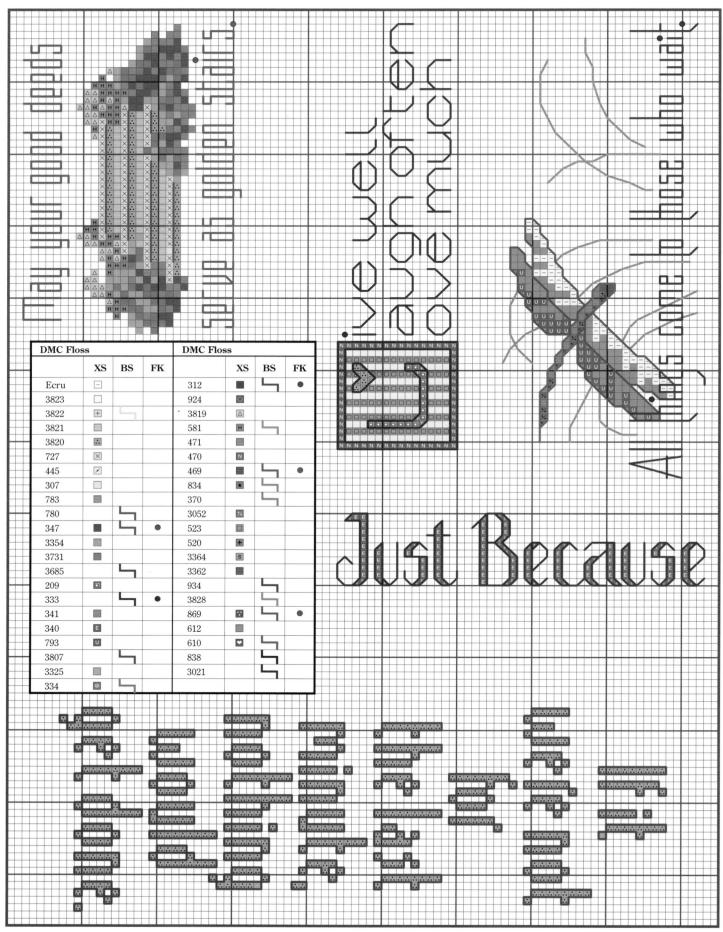

DMC Floss				DMC Floss			
	XS	BS	FK		XS	BS	FK
Ecru	⊟			312	■	⌐	●
3823	☐			924	◉		
3822	⊞			3819	△		
3821	▨			581	H	⌐	
3820	⊡			471	▨		
727	⊠			470	N		
445	◢			469	■	⌐	●
307	☐			834	★		
783	▨			370			
780		⌐		3052	▨		
347	■	⌐	●	523	☐		
3354	▨			520	⊞		
3731	▨			3364	S		
3685		⌐		3362	■		
209	⊡			934		⌐	
333		⌐	●	3828		⌐	
341	▨			869	⊡	⌐	●
340	E			612	▨		
793	U			610	♥		
3807		⌐		838		⌐	
3325	▨			3021		⌐	
334	❀	⌐					

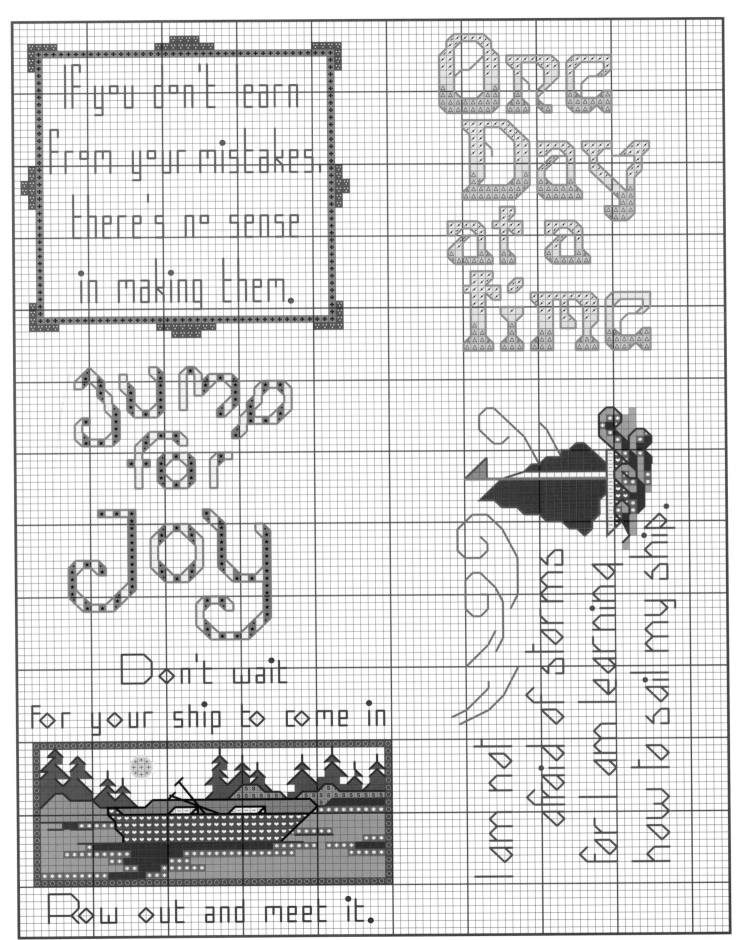

If you don't learn from your mistakes, there's no sense in making them.

One Day at a Time

Jump for Joy

Don't wait

For your ship to come in

I am not afraid of storms for I am learning how to sail my ship.

Row out and meet it.

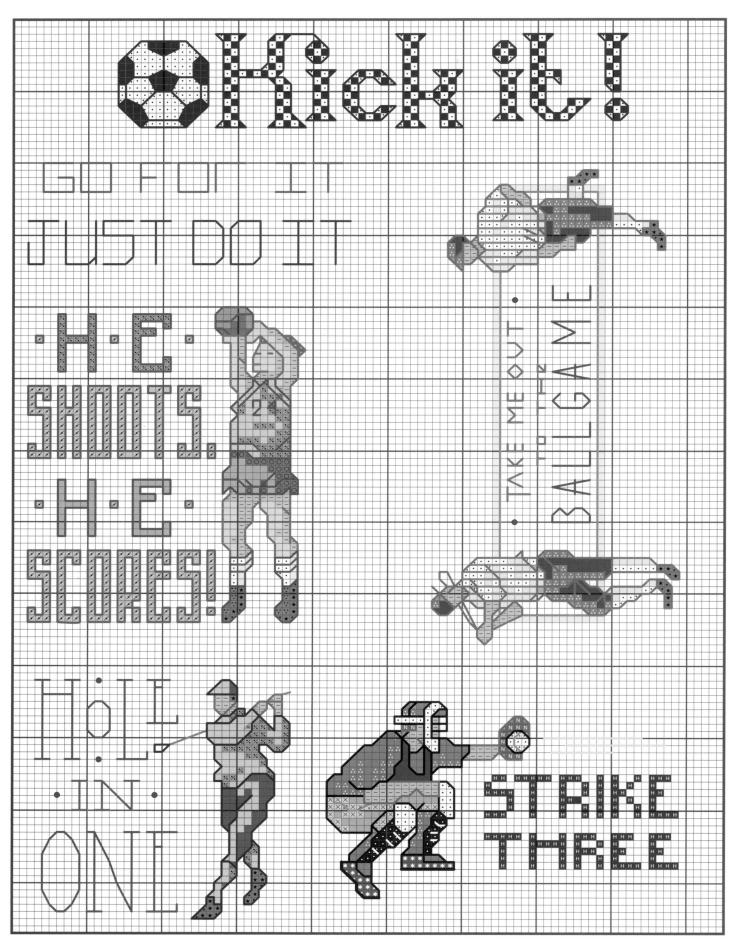

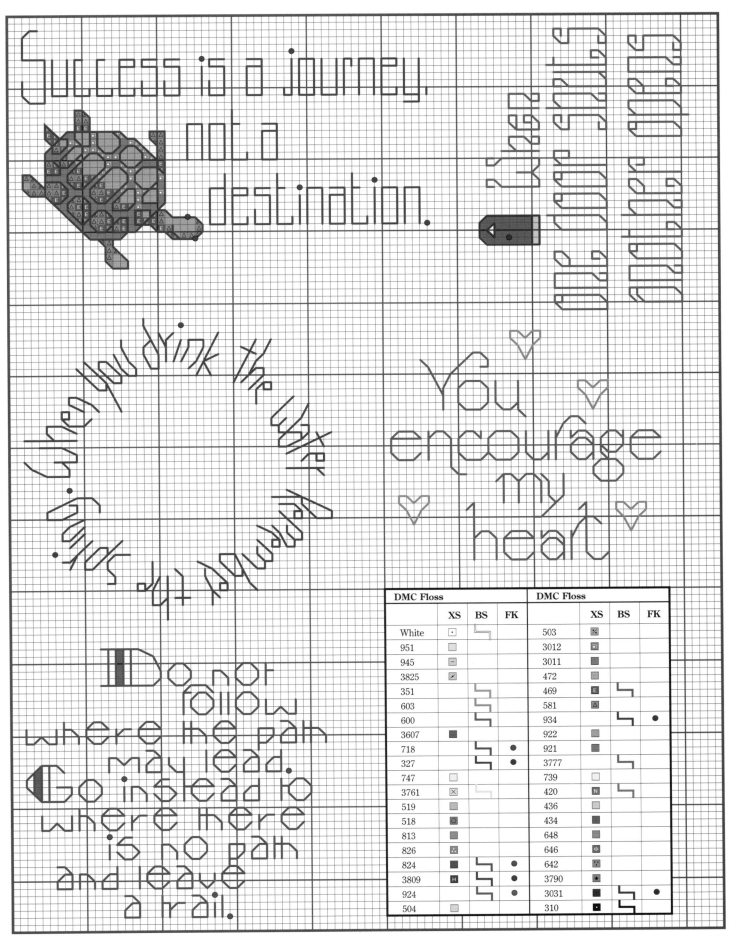

DMC Floss	XS	BS	FK		DMC Floss	XS	BS	FK
White	·	⌐			503	▨		
951	▫				3012	▫		
945	▬				3011	■		
3825	◪				472	▪		
351		⌐			469	E	⌐	
603		⌐			581	△	⌐	
600		⌐			934		⌐	●
3607	■				922	▪		
718		⌐	●		921	■		
327		⌐	●		3777		⌐	
747	▫				739	▫		
3761	⊠	⌐			420	N	⌐	
519	▪				436	▫		
518	◎				434	■		
813	▪				648	■		
826	▪				646	❋		
824	■	⌐	●		642	▪		
3809	H	⌐	●		3790	★		
924		⌐	●		3031	■	⌐	●
504	▫				310	▪	⌐	

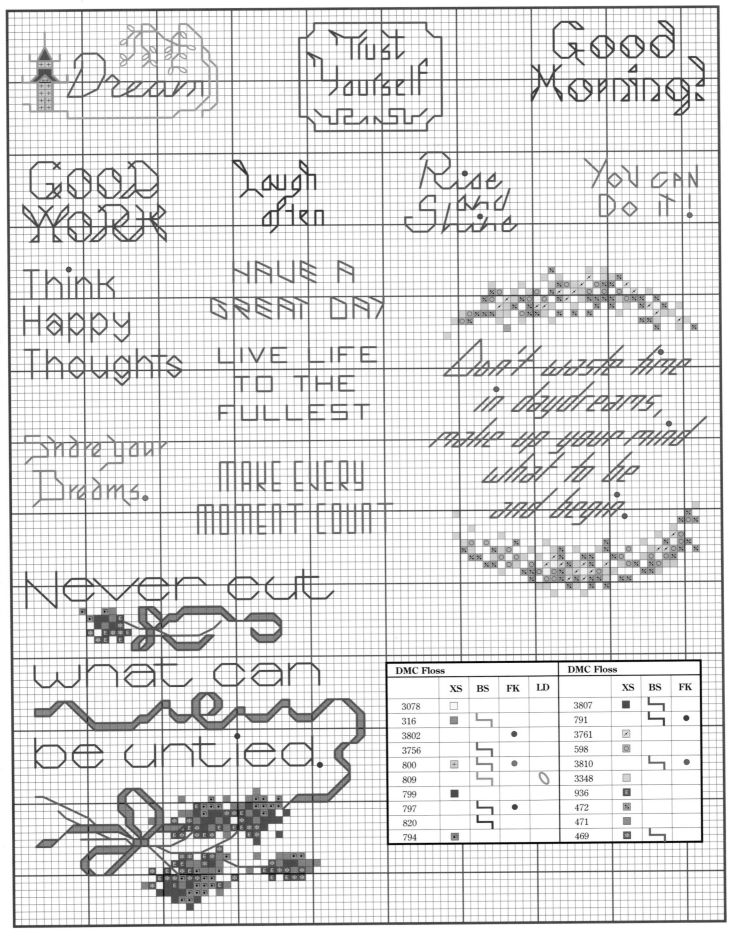

Dream

Trust Yourself

Good Morning?

Good Work

Laugh Often

Rise and Shine

You can Do it!

Think Happy Thoughts

HAVE A GREAT DAY

Share your Dreams.

LIVE LIFE TO THE FULLEST

Don't waste time in daydreams, make up your mind what to be and begin.

MAKE EVERY MOMENT COUNT

Never cut what can never be untied.

DMC Floss					DMC Floss			
	XS	BS	FK	LD		XS	BS	FK
3078	☐				3807	■	⌐	
316	■	⌐			791			●
3802			●		3761	◪		
3756		⌐			598	◉	⌐	
800	⊞	⌐	●		3810	☐	⌐	●
809				◯	3348	☐		
799	■				936	E		
797		⌐	●		472	◪		
820		⌐			471	■	⌐	
794	▣				469	✳	⌐	

Simple Pleasures

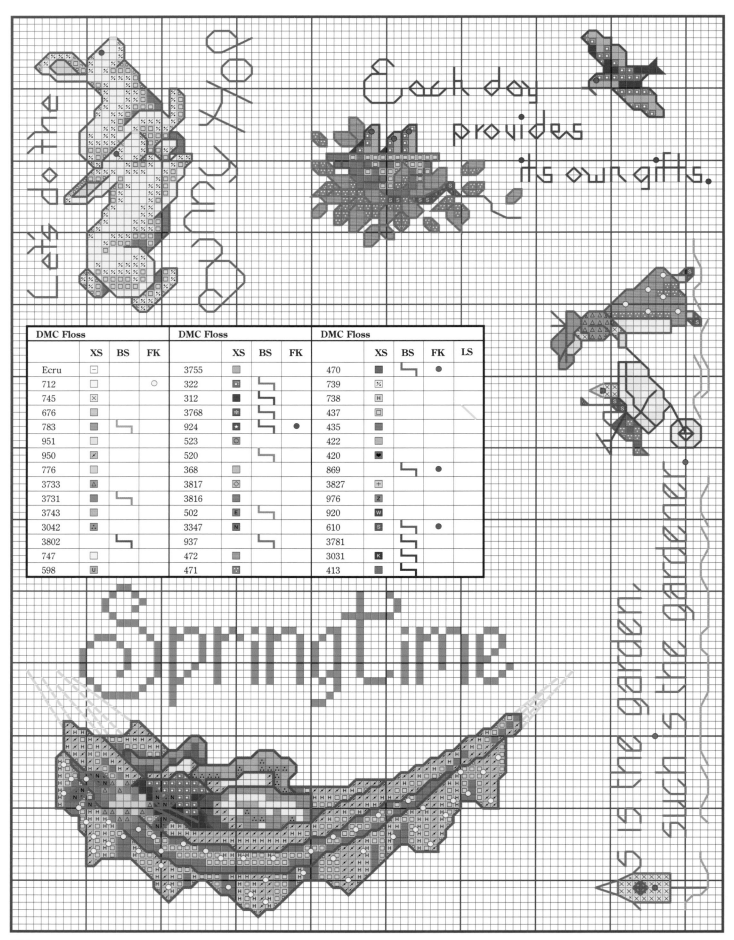

DMC Floss				DMC Floss				DMC Floss				
	XS	BS	FK		XS	BS	FK		XS	BS	FK	LS
Ecru	⊟			3755	▨			470	■	⌐	●	
712	☐		○	322	▣	⌐		739	⊠			
745	⊠			312	■	⌐		738	H			
676	▥			3768	✳	⌐		437	☐			
783	▦	⌐		924	★	⌐	●	435	■			
951	☐			523	◉			422	▨			
950	◪			520		⌐		420	♥			
776	▨			368	▥			869		⌐	●	
3733	△			3817	◈			3827	+			
3731	▦	⌐		3816	▨			976	Z			
3743	▨			502	E	⌐		920	W			
3042	✦			3347	N			610	S	⌐	●	
3802		⌐		937		⌐		3781		⌐		
747	☐			472	▨			3031	K	⌐		
598	U			471	✦			413	■	⌐		

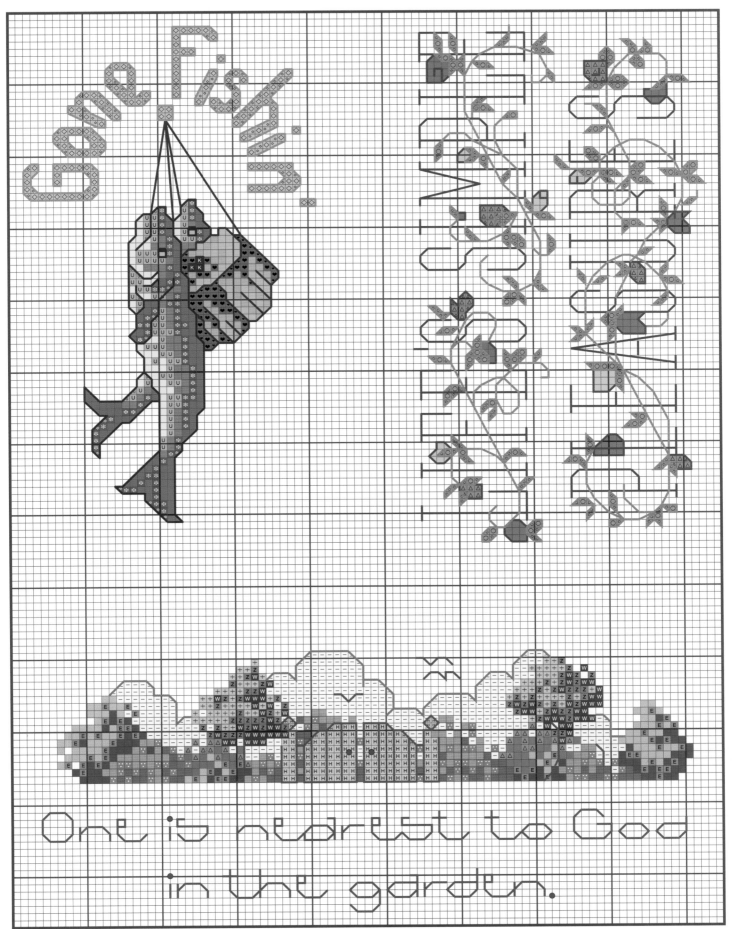

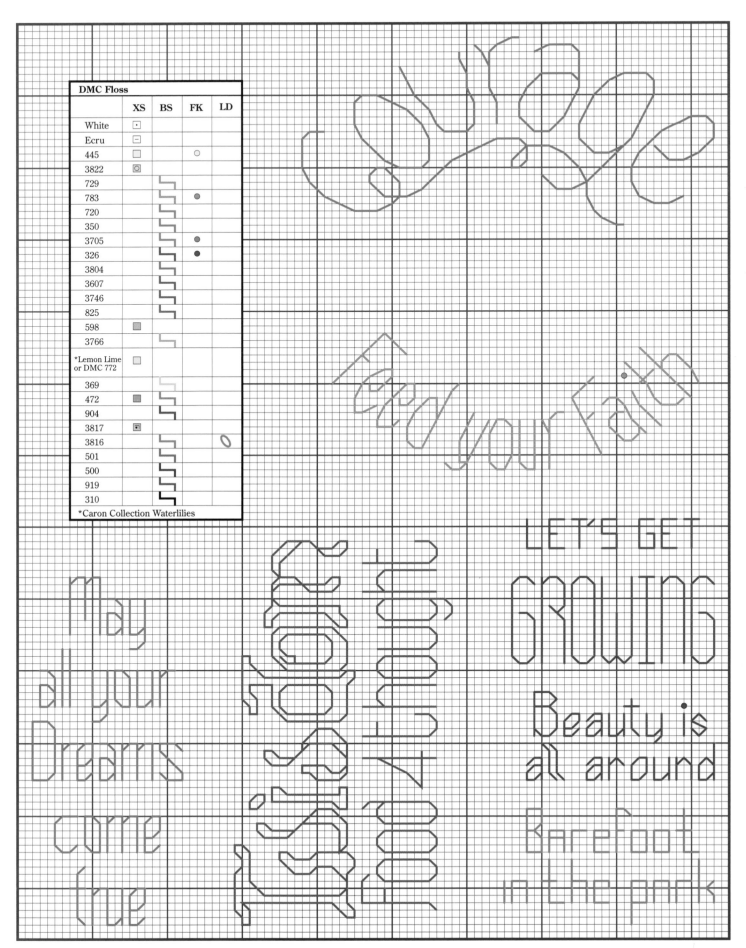

DMC Floss				
	XS	BS	FK	LD
White	·			
Ecru	−			
445	▫		○	
3822	◉			
729				
783			●	
720				
350				
3705			●	
326			●	
3804				
3607				
3746				
825				
598	▪			
3766				
*Lemon Lime or DMC 772	▪			
369				
472	▪			
904				
3817	▣			
3816				○
501				
500				
919				
310				
*Caron Collection Waterlilies				

Garden Party

Make a wish

Spring in the Garden

Harvest Nature's Abundance

Summer

Fall

Spring

Winter

Serenity

Dine on Simple Pleasures

GOD LOVES YOU

THE HOLY TRINITY

Glory

Serenity

We are all GOD's children

Jesus and the Children

PEACE

HEAVENLY SPIRITS

GUARDIAN ANGEL

God bless us everyone

THE LORDS PRAYER

Rejoice

Forgive and Forget

DMC Floss

	BS	FK
5282		
221		●
3041		●
3756 *001BF	>	
3750		●
500		
**2122 or DMC 3772		
***002P or DMC 3829		

*Kreinik Blending Filament
**Kreinik #4 Braid
***Kreinik Cable

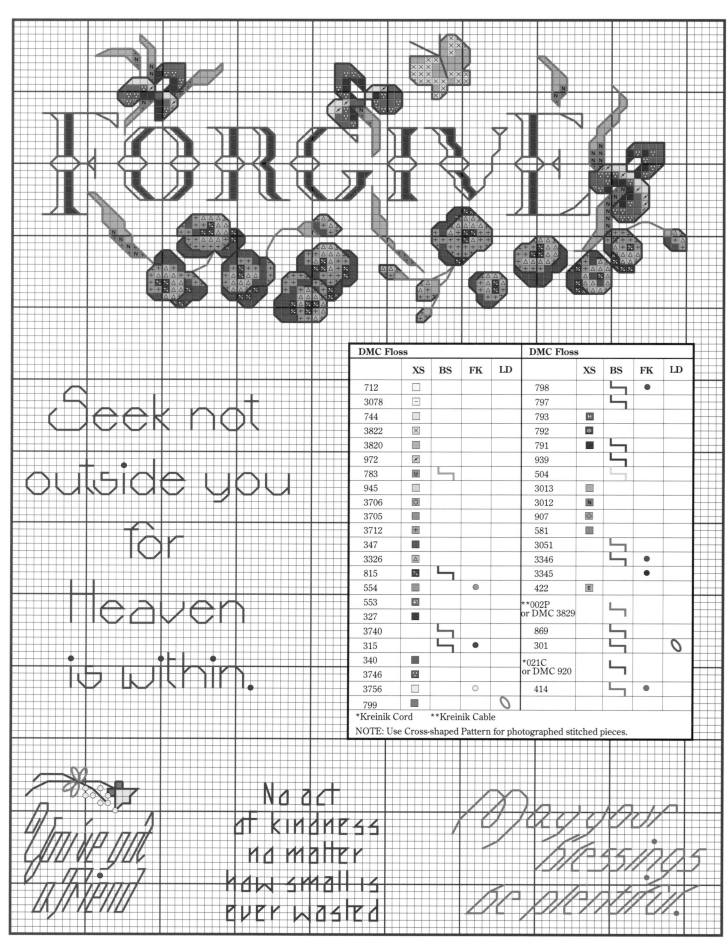

DMC Floss						DMC Floss				
	XS	BS	FK	LD			XS	BS	FK	LD
712	☐					798		⌐	●	
3078	⊟					797		⌐		
744	☐					793	H			
3822	⊠					792	✸			
3820	▦					791	■	⌐		
972	◪					939		⌐		
783	U	⌐				504		⌐		
945	☐					3013	▦			
3706	◎					3012	N			
3705	▦					907	◈			
3712	+					581	▦			
347	■					3051		⌐		
3326	△					3346		⌐	●	
815	▦	⌐				3345			●	
554	▦		●			422	E			
553	▣					**002P or DMC 3829		⌐		
327	■									
3740		⌐				869		⌐		
315		⌐	●			301		⌐		⬭
340	■					*021C or DMC 920		⌐		
3746	▣									
3756	☐		○			414		⌐	●	
799	▦			⬭						

*Kreinik Cord   **Kreinik Cable

NOTE: Use Cross-shaped Pattern for photographed stitched pieces.

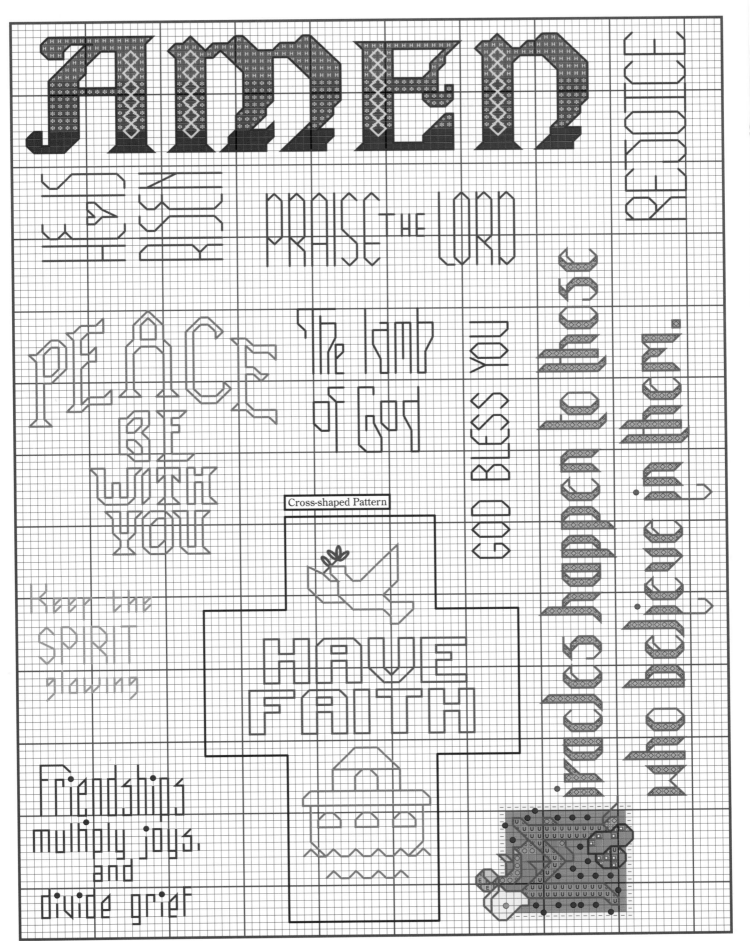

AMEN

HAPPY EASTER

PRAISE THE LORD

REJOICE

PEACE BE WITH YOU

The Lamb of God

GOD BLESS YOU

practies happen to those

Who believe in them.

Keep the SPIRIT glowing

Cross-shaped Pattern

HAVE FAITH

Friendships multiply joys, and divide grief

Keep your treasures
close to your heart

TREASURE
THE MOMENT

Love thy neighbor

A day is lost
if one has not laughed.

day hemmed

in prayer

is less likley

to unravel.

BELIEVE

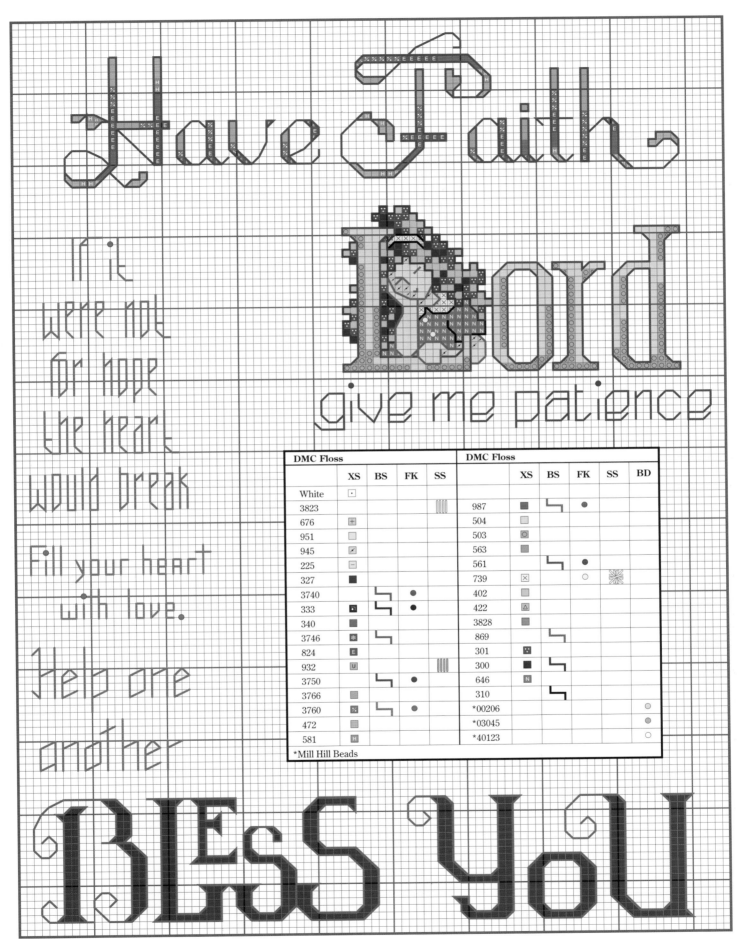

DMC Floss					DMC Floss					
	XS	BS	FK	SS		XS	BS	FK	SS	BD
White	·				987	■	⌐	●		
3823				‖‖	504	□				
676	+				503	◎				
951	□				563	■				
945	◪				561		⌐	●		
225	−				739	⊠		○	✳	
327	■				402	■				
3740		⌐	●		422	△				
333	▣	⌐	●		3828	■				
340	■				869		⌐			
3746	✳	⌐			301	▨				
824	E				300	■	⌐			
932	U			‖‖	646	N				
3750		⌐	●		310		⌐			
3766	■	⌐			*00206					○
3760	▨	⌐	●		*03045					●
472	■				*40123					○
581	H									
*Mill Hill Beads										

109

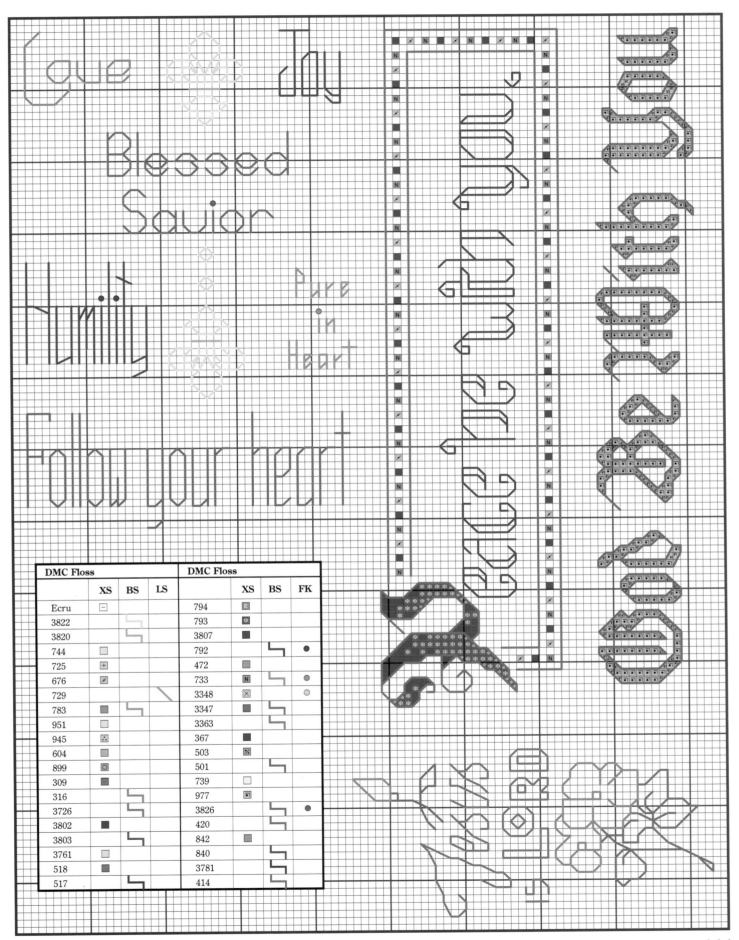

DMC Floss				DMC Floss			
	XS	BS	LS		XS	BS	FK
Ecru	–			794	E		
3822				793	✳		
3820				3807	■		
744	□			792		⌐	●
725	+			472	□		
676	✎			733	N	⌐	●
729				3348	✕		○
783	■	⌐		3347	■	⌐	
951	□			3363		⌐	
945	⊡			367	■		
604	■			503	▨		
899	◎			501		⌐	
309	■			739	□		
316		⌐		977	⊡		
3726		⌐		3826			●
3802	■			420			
3803		⌐		842	■		
3761	□			840		⌐	
518	■			3781		⌐	
517		⌐		414			

Hosanna

Joy to the world

GIVE US THIS DAY
OUR DAILY BREAD

Meek and Humble

This is the day the Lord has made.
Let us rejoice and be glad.

GOD is LOVE

LET THERE BE
LIGHT

Grace

It's more valuable to seek Gods presence than His presents.

GOD ♥ IS ♥ LOVE

Angels among us

Peace in all of the lands. Prayer

DMC Floss			DMC Floss				DMC Floss				DMC Floss			
	XS	BS		XS	BS	FK		XS	BS	FK		XS	BS	FK	LD
White	·		3354	◎			828	⊠			367		⌐		◯
3822	▧		917	■	⌐		3752	⊡			471	△	⌐		
3821	+		3803		⌐	●	930		⌐	●	3053	■			
3820		⌐	3743	▨			517		⌐	●	3345		⌐		
729	■		3041		⌐		797	■	⌐		437	N			
951	−		333	■			336	▣	⌐	●	435	■			
776	▧		775	▧			368	▧			420		⌐	●	

Faith, Hope, Charity

I believe in things unseen

I'M THE WAY, THE TRUTH AND THE LIGHT

Give God Time

Think GOOD DO GOOD BE GOOD

Tranquility

DMC Floss			DMC Floss				DMC Floss		
	XS	BS		XS	BS	FK		XS	BS
White	·		3687		⌐	●	823	■	⌐
Ecru	−		917	■	⌐	●	3053	■	⌐
3822	□		315		⌐		3052	▣	
3821	◎	⌐	340	■			420		⌐
729	■		793		⌐	●			

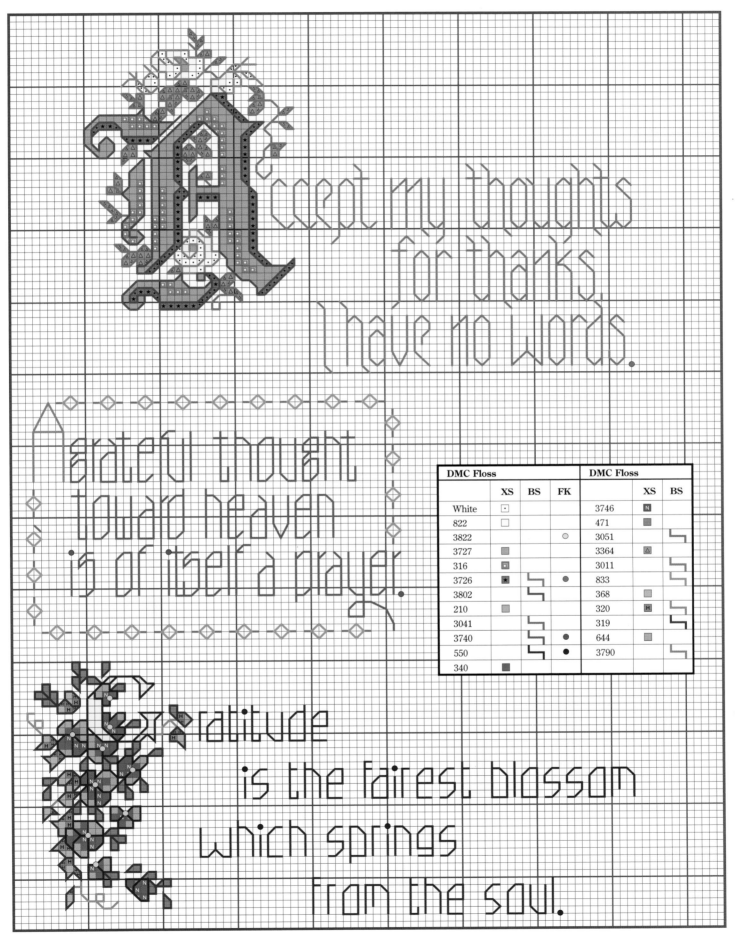

Accept my thoughts
for thanks,
I have no words.

Grateful thought
toward heaven
is of itself a prayer.

DMC Floss					DMC Floss		
	XS	BS	FK			XS	BS
White	⊡				3746	N	
822	☐				471	▦	
3822			◯		3051		⌐
3727	▦				3364	△	
316	⊡				3011		⌐
3726	★	⌐	●		833		⌐
3802		⌐			368	▦	
210	▦				320	H	⌐
3041		⌐			319		⌐
3740		⌐	●		644	▦	
550		⌐	●		3790		⌐
340	▦						

Gratitude
is the fairest blossom
which springs
from the soul.

THANKS A BUNCH

YOU ARE TOO KIND

helping hands

make happy hearts.

Gratitude is when memory is stored in the heart and not in the mind.

Thank You

DMC Floss					
	XS	BS	FK	LD	BD
746	⊟		○		
677	☐				
676	◎				
729	▧				
781		⌐			
951	☐				
945	◪				
3689	▨				
3688	⊞		◉		
3687	◼	⌐			
3685	▩	⌐	●		
340	◼				
3746		⌐			
598	▨				
597	▣				
3809	▩				
3808		⌐	●		
3012		⌐			
472	▨				
471	E				
470	▨				
3051		⌐	●		
937	W				
936		⌐		∅	
402	☐				
3776	▨				
3777		⌐	●		
869		⌐	●		
*2122 or DMC 400		⌐			
632	◼	⌐			
838		⌐			
**62012					●
*Kreinik #4 Braid **Mill Hill Beads					

118

YOUR
KINDNESS
IS GREATLY
APPRECIATED

Instruct me
how to thank thee.

In all things
give
Thanks

Sometimes

I'm overcome

with gratitude.

I wanted someone
to laugh with me -
How do I thank you?

Thank you
for being a true friend

A thankful heart

THANK YOU SO MUCH

Much Obliged

Very Greatful

Thank You
for being a keeper of secrets.

DMC Floss				DMC Floss				DMC Floss			
	XS	BS	FK		XS	BS	FK		XS	BS	FK
**002C or DMC 3820	■	⌐		797	■	⌐	●	503	E		
				823		⌐		3808		⌐	●
3712	■			3813	□			**021C or DMC 356	■	⌐	●
3328	◎			3814	■						
347	■	⌐	●	3348		⌐		*071 or DMC 632		⌐	
814		⌐		***1800 or DMC 581		⌐					
813	⊞										

*Kreinik Blending Filament   **Kreinik Cord   ***Kreinik Ombres

General Instructions

Thread Descriptions

Embroidery floss is a stranded cotton and the most versatile thread available.

Overdyed floss is Egyptian cotton, overdyed by hand, creating a subtle shaded effect.

Waterlilies floss is a 12-ply hand-dyed silk with subtle sheen look.

Where overdyed floss, silk, or specialty threads have been used, a solid color DMC floss has been selected and listed as an acceptable design color alternative.

The threads listed above are distributed by the following:

Anchor (Embroidery floss), 30 Patewood Dr., Greenville, SC 29615

DMC Corporation (Embroidery floss and Metallic floss), 10 Port Kearny, South Kearny, NJ 07032

Kreinik Manufacturing Company, Inc. (Silk floss), 3106 Timanus Lane, Suite #101, Baltimore, MD 21244

Needle Necessities, Inc. (Overdyed floss), 7211 Garden Grove Blvd., Suite B/C, Garden Grove, CA 92841

The Caron Collection (Waterlilies and Watercolors), 67 Poland St., Bridgeport, CT 06605

Simple Pleasures

Introduction

Contained in this book are 555 counted cross-stitch sayings. To create your own one-of-a-kind sayings, vary colors in graphed designs.

Fabric for Cross-stitch

Counted cross-stitch is worked on even-weave fabrics. These fabrics are manufactured specifically for counted-thread embroidery, and are woven with the same number of vertical as horizontal threads per inch.

Because the number of threads in the fabric is equal in each direction, each stitch will be the same size. The number of threads per inch in even-weave fabrics determines the size of a finished design.

Number of Strands

The number of strands used per stitch varies, depending on the fabric used. Generally, the rule to follow for cross-stitching is three strands on Aida 11, two strands on Aida 14, one or two strands on Aida 18 (depending on desired thickness of stitches), and one strand on Hardanger 22.

For backstitching, use one strand on all fabrics unless otherwise specified. When completing a French Knot (FK), use two strands and one wrap on all fabrics, unless otherwise directed.

Finished Design Size

To determine the size of the finished design, divide the stitch count by the number of threads per inch of fabric. When design is stitched over two threads, divide stitch count by half the threads per inch. For example, if a design with a stitch count of 120 width and 250 height was stitched on a 28 count linen over two threads making it 14 count, the finished size would be 8⅝" x 17⅞".

$$120 \div 14" = 8⅝" \text{ (width)}$$

$$250 \div 14" = 17⅞" \text{ (height)}$$

Finished size = 8⅝" x 17⅞"

Preparing Fabric

Cut fabric at least 3" larger on all sides than the finished design size to ensure enough space for desired assembly. To prevent fraying, whipstitch or machine-zigzag along the raw edges or apply liquid fray preventive.

Needles for Cross-stitch

Blunt needles should slip easily through the fabric holes without piercing or stretching fabric threads. For fabric with 11 or fewer threads per inch, use a tapestry needle #24; for 14 threads per inch, use a tapestry needle #24, #26, or #28; for 18 or more threads per inch, use a tapestry needle #26 or #28. Avoid leaving the needle in the design area of the fabric. It may leave rust or a permanent impression on the fabric.

Floss

All numbers and color names on the codes represent the DMC brand of floss. Use 18" lengths of floss. For best coverage, separate the strands and dampen with a wet sponge. Then recombine the number of strands required for the fabric used.

Centering Design

Fold the fabric in half horizontally, then vertically. Place a pin in the fold point to mark the center. Locate the center of the design on the graph. Begin stitching all designs at the center point of the graph and fabric.

Securing Floss

Insert needle up from the underside of the fabric at starting point. Hold 1" of thread behind the fabric and stitch over it, securing with the first few stitches. To finish thread, run under four or more stitches on the back of the design. Avoid knotting floss, unless working on clothing.

Another method of securing floss is the waste knot. Knot floss and insert needle down from the right top side of the fabric about 1" from design area. Work several stitches over the thread to secure. Cut off the knot later.

Carrying Floss

To carry floss, weave floss under the previously worked stitches on the back. Do not carry thread across any fabric that is not or will not be stitched. Loose threads, especially dark ones, will show through the fabric.

Cleaning Finished Design

When stitching is finished, soak the fabric in cold water with a mild soap for five to ten minutes. Rinse well and roll in a towel to remove excess water. Do not wring. Place the piece face down on a dry towel and iron on a warm setting until the fabric is dry.

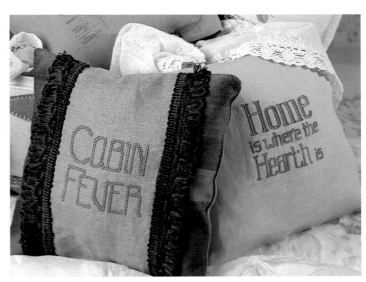

Home & Family

Algerian Eye Stitch (AE)

1. Insert needle up between woven threads at A.

2. Go down at B. Continue around center seven times, bringing needle down through center each time.

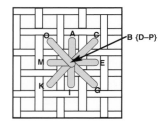

Backstitch (BS)

1. Insert needle up between woven threads at A.

2. Go down at B, one opening to the right.

3. Come up at C.

4. Go down at A, one opening to the right.

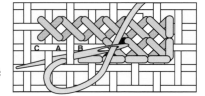

Bead Attachment (BD) and Treasure Attachment (TR)

Beads and treasures should sit facing the same direction as the top cross-stitch.

1. Make first half of a cross-stitch.

2. Insert needle up between woven threads at A.

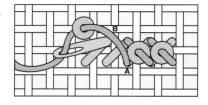

3. Thread one bead before going down at B, the opening diagonally across from A.

4. To strengthen stitch, come up again at A and either go through bead again or split threads to lay around bead and go down at B again.

Cross-stitch (XS)

Stitches are done in a row or, if necessary, one at a time in an area.

1. Insert needle up between woven threads at A.

2. Go down at B, the opening diagonally across from A.

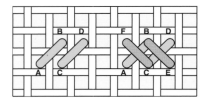

3. Come up at C and go down at D, etc.

4. To complete the top stitches creating an "X", come up at E and go down at B, come up at C and go down at F, etc. All top stitches should lie in the same direction.

Eyelet Stitch (ES)

1. Insert needle up between woven threads at A.

2. Go down at B (center). Continue around center sixteen times, bringing needle down through center each time.

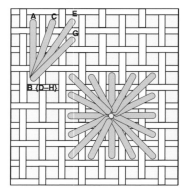

Celebrations

French Knot (FK)

1. Insert needle up between woven threads at A, using two strand of embroidery floss.

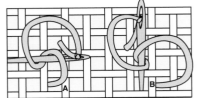

2. Loosely wrap floss once around needle.

3. Go down at B, the opening across from A. Pull floss taut as needle is pushed down through fabric.

4. Carry floss across back of work between knots.

Half-cross Stitch (HC)

Stitches are done in a row horizontally from the left to the right.

1. Insert needle up between woven threads at A.

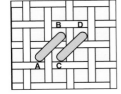

2. Go down at B, the opening diagonally across from A.

3. Come up at C and down at D, etc.

Lazy Daisy Stitch (LD)

1. Insert needle up between woven threads at A.

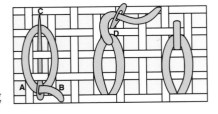

2. Go down at B, using same opening as A.

3. Come up at C, crossing under two threads. Pull through, holding floss under needle to form loop.

4. Go down at D, crossing one thread.

Long Stitch (LS)

1. Insert needle up between woven threads at A.

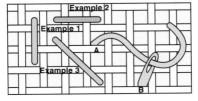

2. Go down at B, crossing two threads. Pull flat. Repeat A–B for each stitch. Stitch may be horizontal, vertical, or diagonal as indicated in Examples 1, 2, and 3. The length of the stitch should be the same as the length indicated on the graph.

Satin Stitch (SS)

1. Insert needle up between woven threads at A.

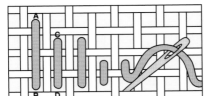

2. Go down at B, forming a straight stitch.

3. Come up at C and go down at D, forming another smooth straight stitch that sits closely to the first stitch, covering the area. Stitches should not overlap.

4. Repeat to fill design area.

Silk Thread Tips

- Strands should be 12"–15" in length.

- Color variation between skeins and bleeding of thread onto fabrics is common with silk thread.

- Silk thread can be combined with cotton thread in the same piece.

- When using variegated strands, cross each stitch as it is made rather than crossing the stitch on the way back across a row.

- Silk cross-stitched pieces should be dry-cleaned rather than hand-washed.

Kreinik Conversion Chart

DMC	= Kreinik	DMC	= Kreinik	DMC	= Kreinik	DMC	= Kreinik
Snow White	Blanc	367	1835/3425	554	3312	725	2514
Ecru	Creme/F2/F13	368	1832/1842	561	146	726	522
208	1334/3335	369	1841	562	144	727	2521
209	1342/3334	370	2214	563	143/211	729	2234/2243/2533
210	3334	372	3833	564	141	730	3724
211	3333	400	4141/4215	580	516	731	516/2214
221	4623/4624	402	632/2622	581	2124	732	2124
223	4622	407	4611	597	132	733	2212
224	4621	413	3445	598	1721/1723	734	2212
225	1011	414	3442	602	3014	738	3821/4112
300	4142	415	3441	603	3013	739	4241
301	2625	420	526	604	3012	740	624
304	943/1026	422	3812	605	3021	741	611/624
307	543	433	4116/4122	606	915/935	742	545
309	2934/2945	434	4516	608	635	743	536
310	Noir	435	4236	610	3835	744	2532
311	1716	436	4235	611	4534	745	2542
312	1715	437	4234	612	3833	746	2541
315	4646	444	536	613	3832	747	1723
316	4634	451	3414	632	4143	754	1012
317	3445	452	3413/3414	640	3834	758	2912
318	3442	453	3412/3413	642	3713	760	2932/2943
319	1845	469	2125	644	3422	761	1013/2931
320	1834	470	245/2125	645	3844	762	3441
321	941/943	471	2114	646	3843	772	2113
322	4922	472	2122/2123	647	1734	775	1441
326	1026	498	945/1026	648	3841	776	2941
327	3315	500	1846	666	915/935	778	4631/4634
333	1344	501	1844/3426	676	2242	780	3816/3826
334	1434	503	1843	677	2141	781	2516/3825
335	3014	504	1822	680	524	782	2244
336	1423	517	1446/1725	699	225	783	2244
340	1343	518	1444	700	226	791	1345
341	1433	519	1442	701	235	793	4913
347	2924	520	3726	702	224/236	794	1434
349	915/935	522	1832/1842	703	223	796	116
350	914/934	523	1841	704	221	797	4924
351	924	524	3423	712	Brut	798	4923
352	932/933	535	3844	718	1043	799	4922
353	921/2913	543	3431	720	634	800	4921
355	2636	550	3336/3315	721	645	801	4115
356	4612	552	3314	722	633	806	126
		553	3313				

DMC	Kreinik	DMC	Kreinik	DMC	Kreinik	DMC	Kreinik
807	125	907	244	973	536	3350	3025
809	1434	909	225	975	4215	3354	3021/3011
813	1443	910	226	976	4212	3362	3726
814	2926/4625	911	214	977	611/2546	3363	1832/1833
815	2925	913	213	986	1845	3364	1831/3723
816	946	917	1043	987	2116	3371	4136
817	916	918	4142	988	2115	3609	1312
818	2942	919	2636	989	234	3685	3026
819	1011	920	2625	991	1826	3687	3023/3024
820	116	921	2615	992	5013	3688	1042
822	3711/3811	922	644	993	1823	3689	3031
823	163/1425	924	205	995	114	3705	914/934
824	115	926	1745	996	113	3706	932
825	1446	927	1744	3011	516	3708	1021/1022
826	113	928	1742	3012	2124	3712	2914
827	1442	930	1715	3013	3722	3713	1011
828	1721	931	1714	3021	3846	3716	3021
829	526	932	1712	3022	3715	3726	4645
830	2214	934	3726	3023	3422	3727	3031
831	2214	935	2126	3024	3421/3841	3731	3013
832	2235	936	2136	3031	4115	3733	3012
833	2233	937	516	3032	4534	3743	3322
834	2242	938	4124	3033	3711	3746	1343
838	4124	939	165	3041	4635	3747	4911
839	3433	945	2632	3042	4633	3750	1716
840	3345/3434	946	634	3045	3742	3752	1712
841	3341	948	2911	3046	2231	3755	112
842	3431/4531	950	2912	3047	2541/2542	3760	1445
844	3844/3846	951	4241	3051	2126	3761	1722
869	526	954	143/211	3052	3723	3765	126
890	1836/1845	955	141	3053	3722	3766	125
891	914	956	1024	3064	4611	3768	1745
893	1014	957	1022	3072	111/1813	3770	F13
894	1022	958	5013	3078	2521	3772	4611
895	1845	959	5012	3325	4921	3774	2911
898	4131/4124	961	3013	3326	3021	3776	644
899	2933	962	3022	3328	2915	3778	2642
900	635/636	963	2942	3340	912	3779	2912
902	2926/4626	964	5011	3341	911	3787	3344
904	2116	966	142	3345	2116	3799	3445
905	224	970	634	3346	2115		
906	223	971	633	3347	2114		
		972	544/545	3348	2113		

Metric Conversion Chart

mm-millimetres   cm-centimetres
inches to millimetres and centimetres

inches	mm	cm	inches	cm	inches	cm
⅛	3	0.3	9	22.9	30	76.2
¼	6	0.6	10	25.4	31	78.7
⅜	10	1.0	11	27.9	32	81.3
½	13	1.3	12	30.5	33	83.8
⅝	16	1.6	13	33.0	34	86.4
¾	19	1.9	14	35.6	35	88.9
⅞	22	2.2	15	38.1	36	91.4
1	25	2.5	16	40.6	37	94.0
1¼	32	3.2	17	43.2	38	96.5
1½	38	3.8	18	45.7	39	99.1
1¾	44	4.4	19	48.3	40	101.6
2	51	5.1	20	50.8	41	104.1
2½	64	6.4	21	53.3	42	106.7
3	76	7.6	22	55.9	43	109.2
3½	89	8.9	23	58.4	44	111.8
4	102	10.2	24	61.0	45	114.3
4½	114	11.4	25	63.5	46	116.8
5	127	12.7	26	66.0	47	119.4
6	152	15.2	27	68.6	48	121.9
7	178	17.8	28	71.1	49	124.5
8	203	20.3	29	73.7	50	127.0

Index